Finding A Voice

American University Studies

Series III
Comparative Literature

Vol. 48

PETER LANG
New York • Washington, D.C./Baltimore • San Francisco
Bern • Frankfurt am Main • Berlin • Vienna • Paris

Marilya Veteto-Conrad

Finding a Voice

Identity and the Works
of German-Language
Turkish Writers
in the Federal Republic
of Germany to 1990

PETER LANG
New York • Washington, D.C./Baltimore • San Francisco
Bern • Frankfurt am Main • Berlin • Vienna • Paris

Library of Congress Cataloging-in-Publication Data

Veteto-Conrad, Marilya J.
Finding a voice: identity and the works of German-language
Turkish writers in the Federal Republic of Germany to 1990/ Marilya Veteto-
Conrad.
p. cm. — (American university studies. Series III,
Comparative literature; vol. 48)
Includes bibliographical references and index.
1. German literature—20th century—History and criticism. 2. German
literature—Turkish authors—History and criticism. I. Title. II. Series.
PT405.V48   830.9'89435043—dc20   92-25758
ISBN 0-8204-2005-0
ISSN 0724-1445

Die Deutsche Bibliothek-CIP-Einheitsaufnahme

Veteto-Conrad, Marilya J.:
Finding a voice: identity and the works of German-language
Turkish writers in the Federal Republic of Germany/ Marilya J. Veteto-
Conrad.–New York; Washington, D.C./Baltimore; San Francisco; Bern;
Frankfurt am Main; Berlin; Vienna; Paris: Lang.
(American university studies: Ser. 3, Comparative literature; Vol. 48)
ISBN 0-8204-2005-0
NE: GT

This book is dedicated with heartfelt admiration and thanks to my parents for decades of unflagging support and love,
and
to my husband for taking this path with me.

My thanks to Dr. Leslie Willson for his wisdom and encouragement.
Zehra ve Kemal'e selam ve sevgiler

I would like to express my appreciation to the following in chronological order of their contributions:

Department of German, University of Texas at Austin
and Freie Universität Berlin
for granting me the exchange fellowship that led to
my choice of research topic

German Academic Exchange Service (DAAD)
for making my further research possible

Heidrun Suhr for her invaluable support
and encouragement

Güliz Kuruoglu for giving me instruction in the
Turkish language

Selver Mengusoglu Wesenack
for her insights regarding her fellow expatriot Turks
and for her generosity in providing me
with lodging in Istanbul

My colleagues at Northern Arizona University
Richard C. Helt, Marie Ingram Helt,
and Nicholas J. Meyerhofer
for their time and their willingness not only to listen
but also to give assistance and astute advice in
completing this manuscript.

CONTENTS

Chapter One

Introduction:
Why Voice?

Turks in the FRG who have chosen writing as their method of
filtering the world around them are a diverse and interesting lot.
When reading their poetry and prose (drama is not the genre of
choice, with the exception of Sinasi Dikmen's satiric plays), the
reader is immediately overwhelmed by the number, intensity,
and in most cases, the quality of what they write. The reader is
also overwhelmed at the thought of trying to classify, to impose
order or a framework around the diversity that is the initial
characteristic of Turkish authors who publish in German. Ulrike
Reeg notes in her study of national minorities in the Federal
Republic that the heterogeneity makes systematization difficult
(12). What do Turkish writers have in common beyond their cultural background? They are both men and women, over fifty and
under thirty, academicians, engineers, cosmeticians, students,
and workers. What could they possibly all have in common? The
answer lies partly in their cultural heritage and partly in the
reception they receive as writers, a dichotomy that forms their
identity.

Turkey is a country with a rich literary history, of which the
Turks are justifiably proud. To view Turkey merely as a struggling third-world nation is to ignore centuries of oral literature
and of written prose and poetry: Diwan literature, Nasreddin
Hoca folktales, and Nazim Hikmet, to name a very few. If Turkey is a struggling nation in the economic sense, in the literary
sense it is firmly established and may rest on laurels that reach
back into antiquity. However, although the Turkish writers in
Germany have this rich heritage in common, their works seem
still in limbo—they are not yet fully incorporated into modern

German literature, but neither are they seen as an outgrowth of the literature of Turkey. They can't be readily pigeonhold into either classification.

The authors themselves question even being classified into any one group. All too frequently the question of their classification has been cloaked in negative terms, such as what they are not, where they are lacking, and where they must be on guard lest they be swallowed up by so-called bona fide German literature. But until now, the obvious and somewhat more positive aspect of this classification question has been completely disregarded—namely that it is precisely this dilemma that piques the curiosity and excites the interest of readers *and* is a central feature of the works themselves: it is the question of identity.

The maintenance of a cultural identity is an essential factor in the lives of Turks in Germany, as well as in the literature written by Turks. Do they have a true *zu Hause*, or home? Can one really speak of the *Fremde*, the strange or foreign land and the state one is in as a stranger or foreigner? Or are both terms relative, albeit frequently evoked?[1] Would the writers who have arisen in Germany have had a voice at all in their home country? Or does the status of otherness, or of distance and estrangement from one's cultural background, afford the necessary distancing not only to the homeland but to oneself as well? How do the writers differentiate between their Turkish selves and their German selves?

The variation and diversity among the writers and their works can be explained in large part by what answers are revealed in their works regarding such questions. By answering the questions, it is possible to understand *Gastarbeiterliteratur*, *Betroffenheitsliteratur*, *Ausländerliteratur*,[2] and all the other less-delineated, but equally important variations and gradations present in the sizable body of literature written by Turks in the FRG.

It is possible to view the development of this particular area of literature in parallel with the stages of human development leading up to adulthood—as a search for identity, a search for a *voice*, here on both an individual and a collective scale. And as with the process of maturation in humans, the process of searching for identity is affected by both inner and outer factors. One outward component reflected in the literature is the political or social factor. This is not to say, however, that these political factors come solely from the German side. Many Turks left their homeland because of the lack of economic stability or political freedom there.[3]

The search of Turkish writers for a voice also has relevance on another plane of identity. The voice they are finding speaks in a tongue other than Turkish. Language differences alienated the first generation of Turks in Germany. The analyses available of first-generation writers' works illustrate what role the alienation played. As Irmgard Ackermann points out in her article "In der Fremde hat man eine dünne Haut," in the case of writers in the second generation of Turks, the isolation is double edged (29). The surroundings they grew up in were predominantly German, but the language of intimacy, of family, remained Turkish. To what extent either resulted in distance is examined in their works. Regardless of generation, the question of language is important, because language manifests identity.

The term *voice* conjures up the image of the voice in song, and in pursuing this metaphor, the question arises: Do Turkish writers in Germany sing a German melody with Turkish lyrics or a Turkish melody with German lyrics? What interdependencies exist, what contradictions, what complements? Finally, is it possible to find a voice, and does that instrument actually express the true essence of what those who possess it, here the writers, hope to convey? Is voice, that is language itself, even capable of conveying it?

In the following chapters, the works of the Turks writing in German are examined in various ways. Each has something to offer in analyzing the writing of Turks in Germany, which can be subscribed under the rubric of the search for a voice, an identity. The process is not complete. It is possible that it may never be completed. But it is undeniably the dominant motif, from within the writers' works, and by dint of the perception that the reading audience has of them, from without as well.

NOTES

1. Cf. Harald Weinrich, *Zeitschrift für Kulturaustausch* 35.1 (1985), 14.

2. Cf. Harald Weinrich,"*Betroffenheit der Zeugen—Zeugen der Betroffenheit,*" *Zeitschrift für Kulturaustausch* 35.1 (1985), 14.

3. Aysel Özakin is but one example.

Chapter Two

Historical Overview
Arbeiter wurden gesucht…

Arbeitskräfte wurden gesucht, Menschen sind gekommen. This statement has become the leitmotiv of all discussions—whether
political, sociological, or literary—surrounding the topic of the
more than four million *Gastarbeiter* currently living in the FRG
and West Berlin. While superficially the statement appears to
seek to be both explanation and apology, in fact it cloaks an
element constituting one fundamental flaw in the manner in
which such discussions are all too often conducted.

For all its apparent pithiness, the statement is patently
untrue in the sense that it reduces the entire situation to pathos.
The fundamental flaw is that most such discussions fall short of
being objective. Of course, workers *were* sought, but it was not
sheer inhumanity that led to the grave shortcomings in the
policy of the Federal Republic—quite the opposite: the all-too-
human error of shortsightedness. Regardless of the current state
of affairs in the Federal Republic, the fact remains that the initial
plan of recruitment did not entail emigration but rather rotation.
That the plan lacked both foresight and an understanding of the
workers' situation is unquestionable and inexcusable. The second section of the chiastic statement is the actual arrowhead on
the shaft of pathos directed at the reader or listener. Depending
on the source, it conveys either self-pity and accusation or self-
accusation and pity. The reduction of the *Gastarbeiter* to poor
sufferers at the mercy of insensitive Germans and their laws may
not be completely off the mark, but the strategy inevitably serves
the purpose of dehumanizing the very group it means to aid.
Once certain groups of foreigners are reduced to a mass, it is
easier to generalize and justify and to avoid the issue of the

position of Turks from the German point of view, because then it becomes "the Turkish problem" instead of the issue for national attention it needs to be. From the Turkish point of view, it is debasing and demeaning to be the focus of pity, because that involves a hierarchical manner of thinking that places the Turks below even well-meaning Germans. The political bottleneck is obvious; the years of unenlightened legislation cannot be dissolved overnight, nor do all areas of government seem disposed to do so. (Think only of the recent popularity of the *Republikaner*, whose party hinges on xenophobia.) The sociological implications are just as complex and overwhelming, but the fact is that the Turks are the leading minority in the Federal Republic, and despite incentives to return to Turkey,[1] most choose an as yet rather bleak future in Western Europe over returning to their native country.

The opening statement, attributed to Max Frisch, seems to say that Turks are not being treated as humans; the exaggeration is useful from a rhetorical standpoint, but one should try to be objective. Turks would welcome equality.

The Turks are a minority in Germany. Many of them also are authors, although most do not support themselves by writing. Does this make their literature a minority literature? Is it a literature of the worker, since the Turks who first came in noticeable numbers were employed in the Federal Republic primarily as unskilled workers? Is it an authentic literature, as women's literature was sometimes called, because it often takes the form of a cri de coeur? How did it arise and how did it develop?

The literature written by Turks initially profited and later suffered from being viewed as a rarefied item. The boom is over, as both first- and second-generation writers concede. Initially the descriptions of the misère of the *Gastarbeiter* were read avidly, but once the element of novelty, of information, of a superficial assuagement of a collective German bad conscience wore off, the audience dwindled, and many publishers balked at continuing to spend money on authors whose works seemed to have lost much of an already small audience. Publishers cannot be faulted, except that they may have been the reason for the short-lived interest by the reading public. The marketing of writers from Turkey or from other lands from which workers were recruited (Yugoslavia, Italy, Portugal, Greece, Spain) had limited usefulness because it proved to be too narrowly defined. The writers themselves reject being relegated to a narrow category of their own, because it limits not only their effectiveness (if indeed their intent is to inform a German audience about Turks) but also their range of audience (if their goal is to be a writer first and only coincidentally a Turk).

Academia, though looked down upon by some writers as being detached from the real and immediate arena of literature, as being a necessarily evil pendant to the infinitely more useful, since living, realm of words, still can perform the ultimate service for the literature of the Turks—and, ironically, by association, to other minority writers, despite the disinclination of most authors to be in a literary ghetto. By adhering to strict, disciplined analysis, and by leaving political and sociological issues aside—for the moment, and granted, artificially—academic study can afford the works of Turkish writers the objectivity they deserve. The early labels of *Gastarbeiterliteratur* and *Betroffenheitsliteratur* prove the point in reverse. While academic critics were focusing only on the political or social status of the writers, their literary worth remained secondary. Now that one speaks of *Migrantenliteratur*, as does Hartmut Heinze in his book by the same name (31), although it is still a label—without which literary criticism seems to feel paralyzed—it is one which allows the literature to be judged on its own merit. One must realize the dangers illustrated with the quote; only then will the literary ventures of the Turkish or Italian or Yugoslav or Chilean inhabitants of the Federal Republic of Germany overcome the barrier of being interesting only as a novelty.

Before an in-depth examination of Turkish writers, it is important to consider them and their compatriots in a historical and political context to fully understand their position. In order to fill primarily unskilled jobs, as Karin König and Hanne Straub document in *Kalte Heimat*, laborers were recruited to work in Germany, beginning with Italians in 1955 (37). By the end of that decade, the demand prompted recruitment contracts to be signed, first with Spain and Greece in 1960, and then with Turkey in 1961. Three years after Turkey was tapped as a source of workers, says Anna Picardi-Montesardo in *Die Gastarbeiter in der Literatur*, the one millionth worker, a Portuguese man, was received with ceremony and fanfare when he arrived by train in Cologne (2). Scarcely ten years later the number of foreign workers and their families had grown beyond the projected number, and a hiring freeze, or *Anwerbestopp*, was put into effect in 1973 to contain their number, which reached its apex that year. But the immigration law, or *Ausländergesetz*, of 1965 had no particular provisions regarding foreign workers' families coming to join their spouses or parents living in the Federal Republic, but rather chose to leave it up to the individual federal states to make their own provisions. For reasons of family unity most states had agreed to allow spouses and children of foreign workers to come to Germany. Many foreigners exploited the regulation and sent for their children shortly before they ceased being minors at the age of eighteen to ensure their residence and hence work permits. The Federal government viewed the practice of sending teenagers as a hindrance to successful integration for several reasons, not the least of which was that many of the nearly adult children often wed in Turkey before departing and then sent for their spouses to come to Germany, too. Thus the number of foreigners increased despite the hiring freeze. On April 1, 1979, the waiting-period decree or *Wartezeiterlaß* was passed as a directive by the Federal Ministry of Labor for the Federal Institute of Labor. As documented in *Kalte Heimat*, the directive declared that members of a family who had come to join their relatives would have to wait a certain amount of time, depending on relationship and age, for their work permit (37). Berlin's Senate declared it to be in the interest of co-existence to avoid yet more foreigners coming to Berlin, and on September 29, 1981 the bill was passed that has come to be known as the Lummer Bill, named for the Senator who sponsored it.

The first of its kind among the states, the Lummer Bill set the immigration age limit at sixteen, required that both parents reside in Germany, and made stipulations regarding the nature and length of the spouse's or parents' stay. The measure may have seemed necessary to stem the influx of foreigners, especially in the light of unemployment figures. Today, much hostile sentiment toward the over four million foreigners is seen as the reaction of disgruntled—though misinformed—unemployed workers who blame the lack of jobs on the foreigners' presence. But the government of the Federal Republic had made the decision to deliberately recruit foreign workers to strengthen the economic upswing in 1955, even, writes Picardi-Montesardo, when the unemployment rate was higher than it was eight years after the hiring freeze of 1973 (1).

Currently, 4.67 million foreigners reside in the Federal Republic. Most have been there for over ten years. Many were born there and know their so-called homeland only as a vacation spot. Of the 4.67 million, 1.49 million are Turkish nationals, who comprise the largest minority group in Germany today. Other nationalities include, in descending order, Yugoslavs, Italians, Greeks, and Poles, as well as several other groups represented in lesser numbers.[2]

Turks are most often the focus of discussions on the topic of foreigners because of their numbers, but also because their country, of all the workers' countries of origin, is the most disparate from Germany. One might argue that Greek culture is also very different from German, but there are merely some two to three hundred thousand Greeks in the Federal Republic as opposed to over a million Turks in Berlin alone. Germans also tend to view Turks as more different because of their religion. Why the Turks tend to be seen as a problem is one aspect addressed by their writing. One argument cited by Picardi-Montesardo to explain German disenchantment with Turks is that Germans are not accustomed to foreigners. However, in the nineteenth century, workers from Poland were recruited to work mines in the Ruhr industrial region; and before the First World War, Turks were employed in German cigarette factories as a result of ties to the Ottoman Empire (3). The term by which such workers were known was *Fremdarbeiter*, a word that was euphemized into

Gastarbeiter and lately into *ausländische Mitbürger*. The first term was at least correct; the latter two terms are euphemistic in that one element is incorrect. A true guest does not work, and a true citizen has actual politic rights.

The fact that Germany has been not only a land of immigration, an *Einwanderungsland*, but also a land of emigration, an *Auswanderungsland*, seems to have been forgotten as well. As Horst Hamm recounts in his book *Fremdgegangen, Freigeschrieben*, Germans have a long history of leaving Germany to seek better work and improved living conditions elsewhere (14-18).

The motivation that led to the Turks' interest in German recruitment stems from similar desires for better-paying work and higher standards of living. Despite the reforms introduced by Kemal Mustafa Atatürk in the early years of this century, designed to Westernize and modernize Turkey, the dual encumbrances of misdirected religious mania and political zeal have curbed the pace of development. Turkey remains a country of contrasts, where the many modern cities are islands in a land whose rural inhabitants often live much as they have for centuries. The East Anatolian Turk who came to Berlin looking for work certainly must have felt like an Appalachian hillbilly in the Big Apple. But the hillbilly does not have the added difficulty of xenophobia, or *Ausländerhaß*, confronting him. As Dr. Hakki Keskin of the Hamburger Fachhochschule für Sozialpädagogik states in *Die Zeit* of January 17, 1986, immigrants are being made the scapegoats for the failure to combat unemployment and the increase of poverty in the Federal Republic. But the foremost flaw in comparing the Turk to a hillbilly is that the hillbilly basically speaks the same language as the New Yorker, whereas the Turkish and the German languages have really only an alphabet in common, thanks to Atatürk's language reform that switched from Arabic to Latin letters earlier in the twentieth century. The analogy to the hillbilly finally falls short when one considers that rural Turks in Germany must confront a new language, yes, and a new lifestyle and a new religion within a culture that was never prepared to truly accept them in the first place.

NOTES

1. For further data, the reader is referred to publications of the Federal Bureau for Foreigners' Affairs in Bonn.

2. Federal Republic of Germany, Commissioner for Foreigners' Affairs of the Senate of Berlin, *Foreign Nationals and Policy of Matters Concerning Foreigners* (Berlin: Federal Republic of Germany, 1985), 1.

Chapter Three

The First Sounds of a Voice
Gastarbeiterliteratur: Ganz Unten?

The first note audible to the public ear, struck in what has since become a complex chord, dealt with the lot of the Turkish worker. Yüksel Pazarkaya, who in 1989 received the Adelbert von Chamisso Prize for contribution of a non-native German to German literature, notes in his essay in the *Zeitschrift für Kulturaustausch*, "Stimmen des Zorns und der Einsamkeit in Bitterland," that almost as soon as they arrived Turks wrote songs of lament criticizing Germany for its treatment of the workers it recruited. Clubs were founded whose newsletters contained poems, stories and dramas in Turkish—the so-called "Germany literature" (17). Writers were addressing the topic of Germany's foreign workers at the same time in Turkey. Pazarkaya himself published a poem in the journal *Yaprak* in Turkey in 1960 about Germany, which was later reprinted in the *Zeitschrift für Kulturaustausch*, lamenting the inhospitability of the country and bewailing the toll it exacts upon its foreign workers, who feed it with their tears (17). And although many of the authors were not, for instance, coal workers in the industrial region of the Ruhr valley, the aspect of the worker still remains a dominant element. Initially, as Pazarkaya notes, the thematization of migration to Germany was a field reserved for Italians (18), because until 1963 no Turks were being recruited. Even as late as 1984, the journal *Sprache in der Gesellschaft* published a volume on *Migrantenliteratur* and *Gastarbeiter* existence edited by Heimke Schierloh, in which only four Turkish authors were listed among eighteen Italians and four others (7-8). CON Verlag's series *südwind literatur* and its active Italian authors Franco Biondi and Gino Chiellino,[1] as well as other minority writers such as Rafik Schami, primarily addressed themselves to the subject of *Gastarbeiterliteratur*, noting the irony of using the two nearly mutually exclusive terms as a compound noun. As Hartmut Heinze notes in his book, the label stigmatized rather than characterized authors (2).

Although both writers and publishers hasten to offer a disclaimer regarding any knowledge of their readership, i.e, audience, reconstruction can be undertaken with the help of newspaper critiques, non-literary publications by the authors themselves, and by considering the number and location of bookstores and the numbers of copies sold there.

The disclaimer spoken almost with one voice by authors and editors, poets and publishers seems for the most part to be at once a defense against a possible critique of pandering to a specific audience (and hence of tailoring one's message) and at the same time a defense against seeming too desirous of an audience. Yet, although a certain amount of artistic freedom is desirable, none of the writers would seek to be published without wanting to be acknowledged, heard: *read*.

At the time when the writing of Turks was marketed and perceived as primarily *Gastarbeiterliteratur* or *Betroffenheits-literatur*, the element of readership and message was straight-forward. The readership, clearly, was intended by the authors to be "the other," the German non-*Gastarbeiter*. (Not all the authors were *Gastarbeiter* themselves, it must be noted.) The strata of society that neither partook of the daily life of *Gastarbeiter* nor even seemed touched by their existence beyond acknowledging the menial labor they performed was to be enlightened. They could have no other audience than a German-speaking one, since their compatriots had no need to be informed about the life of a Turkish immigrant worker. As shall become evident, the audience became a factor that influenced the development of identity with respect to Turkish writers in the Federal Republic.

Lest an impression be conveyed at this juncture that the author's need to express themselves is being relegated to second-ary importance, it should be emphasized that such a need is considered a given: writers write because of the wish to address reality and their perception of it. That this impression and portrayal of reality often influences the reader goes without saying, provided there is a reader. The act of writing involves the reverse of inner contemplation, or *Verinnerlichung*, in the sense that it involves setting down, setting out, or exposing inner thoughts and emotions. Whether the reader agrees or disagrees, the mere act of reading another's perception and description does have an effect. Whether an author intends to influence a reader, indeed whether an author considers a potential reader or not when writing, upon being read the author becomes the transmitter of some sort of message simply by dint of the reader being the receptor of the written word.

And so it was with the texts of *Gastarbeiterliteratur*: By reading about the world of the *Gastarbeiter* in texts such as *Paradies kaputt*, by Aras Ören, the mainly German public received an image of, and a message about the Turks. The economic misery, the cultural confusion, and the crisis of existential identity undergone by the Turks who came to work as unskilled laborers were all laid out before readers.

The members of *PoLiKunst*, which existed from 1980 until 1987, took as their goals the promotion of tolerance and understanding between peoples on all levels of life, and of information about the culture of foreigners in Germany (many of them artists and writers).[2] This they sought to do independent of German control; they allowed German members input, but no voting privileges. A sample of the topics presented at meetings and readings is indicative of the problems faced by all foreigners: "*So sind wir nicht! Das Ausländerbild in der deutschen Öffentlichkeit*" by Turkish satirist Sinasi Dikmen and "*Ein Gastarbeiter ist ein Türke. Zur politischen Lage der Ausländer in der BRD.*"

To their credit, it should be noted that some publishers recognized that the laborer was not the dominant figure in the works of all foreign authors, but it was apparently one that the German public was capable of assimilating into its general world-view, because the books on this particular subject sold very well. The authors were writing a misère, an authentic literature designed to awaken the reading public to the conditions under which the Turkish unskilled workers had to labor, designed to be an appeal for justice. "Authentic" is a label that can be applied to these poems and short prose pieces. They document, as well as Wallraff does in his disguise as a Turk,[3] the burden of societal stigma and of economic and social-underdog status.

Two perpectives on *Gastarbeiter* writings are offered by Aras Ören, an intellectual who was already established as a poet in Turkey before coming to Germany, and Saliha Scheinhardt, a young girl from a strict Islamic village in rural Konya who came to Germany with her German fiancé at the age of seventeen. Both were employed as semi-skilled laborers when they first arrived in Germany, and neither spoke German.

The titles of several of Ören's books, *Was will Niyazi in der Naunynstraße*, *Der kurze Traum aus Kagithane*, *Privatexil*, *Die Fremde ist auch ein Haus*, and *Mitten in der Odyssee*, are themselves like captions to pictures in the life of a Turk who comes to Germany to work and save enough money to return to Turkey a rich man. Although Ören never stated that he identifies himself with the large number of *Gastarbeiter*, he nonetheless chronicles the phenomenon. And since Ören prefers to write in Turkish and then participate in the subsequent translation by a native German rather than writing directly in German, his works are accessible only through the filter of the German language. It is debatable as to whether his initial success was actually due to the quality of the translation by Gisela Kraft.

In *Was Will Niyazi in der Naunynstraße*, Ören begins his panoramic view of a street in Kreuzberg with the life history and thoughts of an elderly German woman, Frau Kutzer. (Kreuzberg is a borough in Berlin where the proletariat traditionally lived. So many Turks now dwell there that the Berlin government stamps into every Turkish passport "*Zuzug nach Kreuzberg und Schöneberg verboten*," that is, moving into Kreuzberg and Schöneberg—the neighboring boroughs—is prohibited.) Through this woman, the reader is given political and social insight into the development of the last fifty years of Germany's existence.

The first third of the book is dedicated to setting the stage via Frau Kutzer. The Turk is introduced in the poem "Frau Kutzers

Nachbarn" and is referred to only as *he*, an Everyman. Thus it is from the standpoint of the German that the reader meets the newcomer. He is portrayed as the victim of a whim of crazy or arbitrary fate. A crazy breeze has twirled his moustache and blown him there (21). The negative imagery of crazy wind, the stereotypically moustachioed Turk, and his irrational, unfounded arrival in Naunynstraße are elements that reinforce the title's announcement that the perspective is Frau Kutzer's. And although the poem proceeds by describing the Turk as decent and reserved, he is nevertheless a scout behind whom his countrymen poured in. And though in the poem Frau Kutzer's attitude seems fairly neutral, after the Turks arrive the street is filled not only with the aroma of fresh thyme but also with fresh hate. Despite the foreboding of this imagery, the final lines of the poem declare that the street called Naunynstraße is what it is because of its Turkish inhabitants (22).

In one of the following poems, titled "Niyazi zieht Bilanz," Ören in one pithy sentence emphasizes the most intangible existential burden of the Turks who came to Germany: being conscious of one's rights inasmuch as one is bereft of them (22).

As the title indicates, Niyazi takes stock; he recounts his life in Istanbul, where he was ashamed of his torn shoes because, although it was his right to live in Bebek, a posh area of the city, he was out of place among the well-heeled inhabitants there. And, like countless others, he saw Germany as a little America, where even the poor lived like the rich did in Turkey. After living seven years in Germany, Niyazi comes to see that his place in society is that of the downtrodden, and as a result he speaks the sentiments of Marx to his listener, whom he addresses as brotherlife—*Bruderleben*. Since the words for love and life are so similar in German, *Liebe* and *Leben,* perhaps this is a nonChristian reference to brotherly love, intended to conjure up feelings of solidarity and community (nonetheless, the references to humans and the earth belonging to them is reminiscent of the Biblical admonition that the meek will inherit the earth) (27). Further indications of Marxist ideology are revealed in the description of Niyazi's girlfriend, whom he met on the Kottbusserdamm boulevard while distributing pamphlets, and who is usually in the front row of any demonstration of Turkish workers screaming that capitalism must go (29).

In a like vein, another figure in this long poem voices a sentiment that glorifies the worker, saying that even a lowly sailor is accorded the title of captain if he saves the ship in rough seas. The speaker, Kazim Akkaya, in referring to the recruited workers who did the menial labor that enabled Germany to function smoothly, here aligns himself with the proletariat attitude of his friends Niyazi and Atifet, though he denies having anything to do with either Rightist or Leftist thought (33). In a similar statement, another friend of Niyazi, Sabri San, reveals an apolitical nature and naïveté, responding to an inquiry about his earning that he saves his money without thought as to why (39).

Sabri San obliquely likens the (Turkish) worker to a *Tret-mühlengaul*, a horse that is made to walk in circles to furnish power for a mill, chained to his task by a harness. Like the horse, the worker is in chains, in invisible handcuffs that only the antidote of drink can loosen for a time (38).

The emphasis on the working class, the common folk, and the inner monologue that makes up the majority of the poems all associate Ören with Brecht. The characters' statements are a tirade against a society that mistreats those who help it function, a society that is rife with faults. Interestingly, Ören depicts the ills of society, but he chooses to portray them in the example of a German worker, Klaus Feck, rather than in a more stereotypical character from upper-class Germany, and in doing so adds a deeper level of poignancy and bitterness to his view of the flaws in German society. As in real life, it is the worker who becomes so frustrated that he turns on his Turkish counterpart; the workers are divided by strife, the common denominator which—being the downtrodden class—by rights should unite them against the hierarchy that instigated the injustice. After years of hearing slogans crying for protection of democratic order (47) as the underpinnings of materialism, Klaus goes mad, disillusioned by hypocrisy, and disassociates himself from all his political ideals, crying that they have gotten him nowhere (47).

The end of the poem takes a twist: Klaus's crazy tirade takes place in a pub, where he sits drinking beer with Kirsch chasers. It is in the pub that, in his impotent rage, he drunkenly lashes out at a foreigner. The bitter significance of his tirade lies as much in its content as in the audience who hears it: The men listening to Klaus sport tatooes and polished shoes. Ören adds to the ominous description by describing the men's inner trappings, too: heads whose thoughts nourish a poison-spitting snake. These men all agree with Klaus, are happy about his madness. Ören describes what they lack—machine guns, steel helmets, boots and brown uniforms—but it is clear that they are the Neo-Nazis, those who foster German discontent in the hopes that the discontent will one day be directed at non-Germans. As in Brecht, the ignorant are obviously the most dangerous, regardless of class.

Ören does not permit the German reader the luxury of putting the blame on Neo-Nazis alone; in the short cycle of grievance poems of *Mitten in der Odyssee* titled "Klagen Beschwerden Lieder Darstellungen der Unsrigen in Berlin," he speaks broadly of *us* and *them* (85-94). The third of six poems, "Beschwerde der Unsrigen in Berlin in zwei Variationen" (90-91) is an unbridled accusation that condemns German society for viewing the Turkish workers as egg-laying chickens cooped up in stalls of barracks euphemistically called living quarters (*Wohnheime*). The poem contains a reproach to German employers for indifference and brutality in answer to the workers' productivity and patience. A further reference to Brecht is the allusion to the worker as a cog in the wheel of production. It is also a warning that the *Gastarbeiter* will not allow themselves to be exploited forever (91).

Ören, of all the Turkish writers, is the one whose texts about *Gastarbeiter* most resemble actual proletarian literature. For the most part, however, the universality that underlies true workers' literature is not a component of the *Gastarbeiterliteratur*. Thus, as Heidrun Suhr points out, it is not to be categorized as proletarian literature. She refers to Franco Biondi, a spokesman for international authors, who also rejects the view of foreigners' literature as merely a part of proletarian literature (562).

Claudio Lange's international *Literaturgruppe*, in the seventh of their list of fifteen demands, called for the label *Gastarbeiterliteratur* to be eliminated as soon as possible from bookstores and libraries, saying in the *Loccumer Protokolle* that nationality of the writer or poet does not automatically classify him or her as a writer of *Gastarbeiterliteratur* (137).

NOTES

1. Biondi and Chiellino were founding members of the now-defunct society of foreign writers and artists in Germany: *PoLiKunst*, the *Polynationaler Literature - und Kunstverein*.

2. Cf. Alev Tekinay, "Fünf Jahre PoLiKunst." *Bizim Almanca/ Unser Deutsch* 9.2 (1985), 35–36.

3. Günter Wallraff infiltrated a company disguised as a Turk in order to write an exposé, *Ganz Unten*, on German firms' hiring of illegal *Gastarbeiter*.

Chapter Four

Voice As Identity:
"Zwischen zwei Stühlen"

What does a Turk write? Can an inherently Turkish metaphor be said to exist? In short: Does the body of works by Turkish authors writing in the language of another country, Germany, reflect a collective consciousness? These are questions not easily answered, since the definition of collective varies from one author to another. Judging by the large number of authors at conferences such as the March 1988 Literatur im interkulturellen Kontext in Iserlohn, sponsored by the Evangelische Akademie, the answer is yes: Authors from all parts of Germany convened to discuss the role of their literature and the reception of non-native German-language poetry and prose by a German reader-ship. Despite individual differences, all in attendence, whether Turk, Chilean or American, expressed a common bond in their mutual otherness.[1] The bond really stemmed more from the reception of these authors as being different rather than from an inherent commonality among them; when the talk turned to mutual experiences, generally it revolved around how to utilize and not be stigmatized by being different from mainstream German authors. The authors of foreign extraction did not actively seek to totally separate themselves from the German literary scene, but the question must be raised: Did they not convey, albeit unintentionally, a collective image?

In *Kulturelles Wirken in einem anderen Land*, published in the *Loccumer Protokolle*, Aysel Özakin speaks for many of her fellow Turks in the article "Ali Hinter den Spiegeln" (32). She recounts seeing the Wallraff bestseller *Ganz Unten* in every bookstore window and feeling as if all of Germany saw only unskilled, un-derprivileged workers when they visualized a Turk. Wallraff's book was initially a bestseller and then a scandal when it became apparent that he exploited Turkish colleagues[2] in order to write a version of the 1960s book *Black Like Me*. In *Ganz Unten*, he (a German) masquerades as a Turk in order to reveal the foul dealings of huge firms hiring illegal aliens. Özakin speaks of her involuntary self-identification with any other Turk on the street. She finds it disquieting, limiting of the personal freedom she remembers in Turkey, when she could view her society with critical eyes. Her words reveal a realization that like it or not, she speaks for the collective whole, though she writes as an individual. She sees the function of an artist who comes from a proletariat background as a tool to give voice to the masses. Similarly, Turks writing in the Federal Republic cannot be outside the social reality of their working countrypeople.

Still, she rails against the categorization that causes (presumably her own) works to land in cases marked "Gastarbeiter" in bookstores, of interest only to social workers, teachers, and students writing theses. She asks why no one assesses such works for their literary value, rather condescendingly relegating them to mere pedagogical or didactic use in the classroom (37).

In answering the question of a collective image, it may be useful to turn the tables and view the German reading public, rather than the authors and their subject matter, as a collective. Except for Ören's works, primarily in the form of anthologies published by for example the well-known German paperback publishing house Deutscher Taschenbuch Verlag (abbreviated as dtv), did these texts sell so well because buying (and presumably reading) texts by and about *Gastarbeiter* served as a sort of collective therapy for Germans? Did the attempt to inform oneself via such texts about the relatively new realm of German society serve as a catharsis, an assuagement, of some collective guilt? Individual writers and publishers contend that this is the case,[3] and attribute the drop in sales to the end of the cathartic experience, as if the public as a whole was saying to itself, "We have done what we could by reading about them, we are now enlightened and have no need for further action because since we sympathize and have read the books, we are not to blame for the status of Turks in the Federal Republic." If this is actually true, then it is yet another indication that the "ghettoization"— *Ghettoisierung*—that occurred with regard to the level of living accommodations for Turks has reached into how the writers were marketed and how they were generally perceived by readers. Although addressing the status of the guest workers was laudable, it reinforced the tendency to focus on the Turks as downtrodden.

Even Günter Wallraff's account of his two-and-a-half-year masquerade as an illegal Turkish worker had negative repercussions despite its phenomenal sales—550,000 in the first week alone. Both of the aforementioned accusations by former Turkish co-workers and the satiation effect of watching exposé upon Walraff exposé reveal yet another flaw in German society detracted from his book's hoped-for impact. A negative image unwittingly perpetrated by Turkish writers who sought to depict the everyday situation of foreign workers persists today and causes authors who do not address the issue of *Gastarbeiter* to grapple with publishers who hope that by resurrecting the topic, they might engender more appeal.[4]

Interestingly, the initial emphasis by both authors and publishing houses on the *Gastarbeiter* phenomenon has led some newer authors to take the opposite tack in some of their poems. The following poems, all but one from the dtv anthology *Türken deutscher Sprache* bear witness to the complexity of levels involved even in the *Gastarbeiter* texts that have often been scorned as too message-bound, not literary enough. Although the poems by Senocak, Kurt, and Zehra Çirak speak of the *Gastarbeiter*, they do so in the multi-faceted, condensed, and evocative manner that is characteristic of any poetry of high literary quality.

Zafer Senoçak is a younger poet of the second generation of writers. His poem "Du bist ein Arbeitsknochen," published by dtv in *Türken deutscher Sprache*, is a densely woven tapestry of expectation, emotion, confusion, and fact, all combined to depict the situation of the *Gastarbeiter*, and to convey his (initially the *Gastarbeiter* were only men) background as well as his current position. In it, Senoçak attacks the prevalent image of the

Gastarbeiter. The tone is matter-of-fact, not lamenting or maudlin, and therefore the poem cannot be classified as a poem of misère or victimization; no poem of *Betroffenheit*. The *du* address, although familiar, is neither belittling nor brotherly; rather it conveys the "everyman" aspect of the phenomenon of *Gastarbeiter*, and at the same time his anonymity; this person, though called by the informal *du*, is not given a name. The anonymity also underscores the status of the *Gastarbeiter* in his work milieu: He is a function, not a personality. The careful, almost textbook-like tone of the poem does not exclude human emotion, but it, too, is portrayed behind laconic factual statements—likening helplessness to feeling like a squeezed-out lemon (89)—that only hint at the depth of suffering. Perhaps the bald factuality is a reflection of the suppression of strong emotion necessary as a defense mechanism when one's lot as a foreign worker becomes too overwhelming. More likely, it is the voice of one close enough to understand, one who hopes to point out the pitfalls of defining one's identity via one's professional status. This epithet can become a millstone. In Senoçak's implied criticism he expresses sympathy, but he refuses to subjugate himself, merely because he too is a Turk, to the identity of a subhuman worker.

The voice represents lament, indignation, a literary call for change. The question of identity is a different one altogether. Did the cry from the heart, the accusing finger pointed at German society in these texts, achieve the goal of diminishing prejudice and inequality or did it further cement the negative image, making self-fulfilling the very problems to which it addressed itself? The publishers began to directly request from those authors whom they sought out for publication an image of the down-trodden, whose lament had been selling so very well, and the authors found themselves locked into a collective stereotype that they themselves had unwittingly helped create. As Eberhard Seidel-Pielen writes in the Berlin magazine *zitty* of June 1989, publishers vied for foreigners who would write about their dismal experiences in Germany. One anthology after the other was tossed onto the market. After twenty years the Federal Republic discovered that 'its' foreigners could also read and write (17). The earlier anthologies are marked primarily by the brooding voice of the underdog.

The first of several anthologies that were the results of liter-ary contests sponsored by the Institut für Deutsch als Fremd-sprache in Munich was the dtv's 1982 publication, *Als Fremder in Deutschland*, which served as the springboard for several writers, among them Zehra Çirak and Kemal Kurt. The anger, resigna-tion, bitterness, and sorrow inherent in these poems is an appeal for reform, or at least for understanding, as typified in the poem "Sehnsucht" by Hatice Kartal and Hülya Özkan. It is a lament for the homeland, a voice grieving for what is lost and what is missing in the new country. The speakers tell of poverty that has driven them to a strange country to work that decimates them. Unlike many texts dealing with *Gastarbeiter* existence, however, the voice of the poem by Kartal and Özkan lays much of the blame for present misery on itself. The narrators berate them-selves for being blind to the advantages of the homeland, for not having loved the homeland sufficiently. The text, spoken to the personified Turkey, is full of expressions of poverty, slavery, sorrow, homesickness, and regret.

Love for Turkey is frequently a motif, but self-destructive guilt about a situation in which one actually is a victim is very unusual. More typical is an accusatory tone, such as in Sühan Sen's poem "Einladung." In the poem he appeals to, even challenges, the addressee to dare to become involved. The one issuing the challenge lists the reasons why he is worthy of involvement, of interest, and the positive reasons are the mirror image of the actions of xenophobic Germans. The plea is to be able to live with dignity in a country many see as synonymous with culture. The plea contains an accusation too, since it states that dignity is only possible with humans. The poem ends in anguished bewilderment, asking why, if Germans look like Turks, are they so blind? (117). An intriguing angle is given to the reader who is permitted to see the question of integration from its other slant. Though the blame for inadequate interming-ling of Germans and Turks is frequently placed upon the Turks' cultural "otherness," here the mirror is held up to the Germans' flaws. From the viewpoint of the Turks, they are confronted with a style of interaction that is so foreign as to cause them to wonder what manner of people these Germans are.

A year after the first anthology was published, a second one appeared from the same publishing house, supported by the same institute, titled *In zwei Sprachen leben*. A slightly larger volume, it was also a collection of prose and poetry by writers of various nationalities. Many authors express gratitude for the opportunity to be published that is afforded to them by the dtv, but the compilation, some now argue, led the reading public to a less than subtle view of non-native German writers.[5] The tone as a whole is also slightly changed; the accusatory timbre is quieter, and self-criticism, often undertaken by second-generation Turks, plays a definite part, as in the short prose text by an anonymous author who styles himself or herself HSM. In it, the writer speaks of the pull exerted by both cultures on a young Turk in Germany, the linguistic difficulties, and the efforts at enlightenment and at dismantling prejudices. Yet, says the writer, young Turks belong to a minority that is acknowledged by no one, and, consequently, they lose hope of being anything but foreigners both in Germany and at home in Turkey; a tree with leaves and branches but without roots.

The second anthology's authors seem to be moving away from the strategies of those in the first anthology (or perhaps the perception of the situation of foreigners led the editors to choose a different perspective), toward a more productive, because more realistic goal, tackling the chore of adaptation rather than mere protest. Oral Yilmaz, not himself a second-generation Turk, in his poem "Die zweisprachige Welt" (44) addresses the need to find means to survive. He has his personae, three fathers worried about their sons' faulty bilingualism, speak of the need to communicate in the bilingual world, and their desire to make it easier for their sons. The closing line states simply the difficulty of communicating in a bilingual world (45). This statement takes on dual meaning: The world the sons live in requires them to straddle two cultural and linguistic arenas, yet the two disparate paternal and filial worlds create a generation gap of experiences not shared that make it impossible for the fathers to speak words of advice to their sons.

In the second anthology, one pivotal element that strikes the reader is the emphasis on language, which is obvious from the title itself. As in Yilmaz's poem, a short prose piece by Özgür Savasçi, "An einem Freitagabend" (92), focuses on the dilemmas about language with which a near-bilingual foreigner's existence is fraught. After rescuing a girl being pursued by a man she met in a disco, three Turkish men escort her safely home. On the way, "Translator" (*Dolmetscher*)—so-called by his countrymen for his bilingualism—lists in his mind the possibilities for striking up a conversation and rejects each one after imagining the various ways in which they could be misconstrued by the girl, if she were inclined to be suspicious of foreigners. The entire short story deals with language, for even prior to the incident with the girl who is harassed, the narrator soliloquizes on the theme of the idioms for "tipsy" in German and Turkish; a further manifestation of the sensitivity for both languages apparent in the second of the dtv anthologies. As shall become evident, this is also an indication of Turkish authors' broadening their readership's sensibilities for language by opening up the vista of a language that otherwise might be closed to them, namely Turkish.

Hülya Özkan, a name familiar from dtv's first anthology of foreign writers, writes in the second anthology of "Zukunft ohne Gegenwart," in which language plays a devisive role where the gap between nationalities and culture cannot be bridged (111). Like her countryman Sabri Çakir in "Ich habe zwei Heimatländer," she deals not only with language, but with the nationalities and cultures that convey their individuality by, among other means, language. Çakir speaks of having two faces: one for Germans, the other for his countrymen (126).

Yet another writer, Ertunç Barin, compares living in two languages to trying to walk in a single shoe into which two feet must fit simultaneously (127). The main character in Alev Tekinay's short story is a young Turkish worker who tries to avoid the pinching of the shoe. After a year in Germany, he meets a Turkish woman who teaches him German and he determinedly sticks to German even when the teacher seeks to revert to their mutual tongue, with the justification that not only does Turkish fail him, but that one should speak the language of the country (133). This young man, named Ali, perhaps because for Germans the generic name for Turks is Ali, just as the collective or generic Russian is called Ivan, this Everyman—*Jedermann*—is the *Gastarbeiter* who hasn't an accusation to make, whose German is virtually without accent, and who voluntarily translates his surname Yildiz into its German equivalent, Stern. He has a job, but it causes him eye trouble, and his attempt at joviality is strained. He exits, leaving his erstwhile teacher to muse that the difference between him and her is that she has a purpose in life: teaching such newcomers as him to survive in a country that may prove to be their undoing in the long run.

Just as the language school gave the student Ali the skills that eventually make him useful to employers in less-than-favorable work situations, so too does the high school give the narrator in Birol Denizeri's story "Tote Gefühle" (176) the means to understand the hateful Turk jokes with which his classmates taunt him. The so-called tools of integration, education and language, are revealed as double-edged swords that can potentially be wielded by Germans to cause distress. Cengiz Kip turns this sword over to Turks in his short story "Fahrt der Hoffnungen" (198), in which a bilingual Turk protects a naïve countryman by falsely translating the answers the latter gives to immigration officials. A second contribution by Alev Tekinay to the anthology, *Langer Urlaub* (203), highlights a different side of language, saying that she cannot always tell which is the so-called mother tongue and which is the second, or daughter, tongue (204).

Does this feeling that language is independently taking over, acquiring a life of its own, transfer to identity as well? In his pensive essay, "Hängebrücke" (218), Ihsan Atacan says it makes one a more careful person when one wishes to be accepted in a second language, and that it takes courage to attempt to do so. Why courage? Probably because to adopt another language is to rearrange, even drastically alter, the constituent parts of one's self-image. To adopt a language inherently involves some de-

gree of adaptation to a culture. Why would taking on facets of
what it means to be German present such difficulty?

To answer that question, it is helpful to inspect the image of
Germans and Turks in the literature of the non-German minority
writers. The third in the series of dtv anthologies, published in
1984, makes this objective easier, since it concentrates exclusively on Turks, hence the title *Türken deutscher Sprache*. As was
the case in the first two anthologies, many of the writers featured in *Türken deutscher Sprache* have since become well known
as writers; nearly two-thirds are established authors. Since the
third anthology is devoted exclusively to authors of Turkish
extraction, it lends itself readily to the self-portrayal of Turkish
nationals and to an assessment of the image of Germans in the
eyes of Turks.

Evident in most of the poems, and especially characterized
by the first poem of the anthology, Hasan Dewran's "An den
Ufern des Euphrat" (11), is the deep sense of devotion to home.
Dewran's evocation of the river Euphrates as a source from
whence comes a vast outflowing is symbolic for the exodus of
Turks from their home country to Western Europe. The anthology continues in a like spirit with several texts of an autobiographical nature that nonetheless further develop the theme of
home and native culture via depictions of village and family life.
Non-rural settings are also described, as is the reaction of Turks
meeting the first German ever to arrive in their village. Poignant
accounts of the disruption of an age-old cultural milieu round
out the picture of Turkey and allow the reader the most telling
insight of this anthology: Turkey is in the throes of progress, and
the price of progress is often pain, as is clearly depicted in Deniz
Çaliskan's "Abschied." She describes the scene when leaving for
Germany after a vacation in Turkey as a final holding fast to the
intact world and a putting off of the unpleasant (33). When she
leaves, the Turkish music fades and dies and childrens' voices
are lost in the distance as she approaches what she views as a
time of sorrow and loneliness (34). The sense of allegiance to
one's own culture and home country is one possible reason for
the displacement many authors in this anthology express in

poems such as Zafer Senocak's "Doppelmann." The first-person narrator tells of having his feet on two different planets, whose orbits diverge and cause him to fall. The two worlds are internal, as well. Neither is whole, indeed they bleed constantly. The border of these divided worlds, internal and external, is manifested in his tongue. The tongue is divided, painfully so, yet he cannot leave it alone for it to heal (39).

Those Turks who still have strong ties to their home villages notice a sense of displacement in a foreign country; to those who may have grown up in Germany, the ties to Turkey are less strong, which leaves them feeling alienated in both countries. Since they are fully articulate in neither language, for them their tongue symbolizes a border, a division they are struggling to overcome. A seeming exception are the two Germanophiles who view their country from the outside after having become acculturated in Germany but who return to Turkey for professional reasons in Alev Tekinay's story "Die Heimkehr oder Tante Helga und Onkel Hans" (40). They see Turkey as Germans would and are discontented with its backwardness, its weather, and the fixed roles for men and women. Like inflexible tourists they search frantically for "real" food in a strange land and relish the care packets from German friends. Like tourists, they find joy mainly in sightseeing, since it provides them with material for letters to their German friends. Yet, when they can no longer stand their homesickness for Germany and decide to go back to Munich, they suddenly begin to recall aspects of German life that they have always despised or that they suddenly find themselves despising: punctuality, unfriendliness, indifference, cleanliness, and most of all the feeling of being different, of not belonging (51). When a taxi driver mistakes them for Germans returning from a vacation in Turkey and asks "Back home?" they smile that yes, they are, but ponder whether the term *home* can really be defined (51). The first exclusively Turkish anthology in the dtv series is therefore remarkable for the disparate nature of the self-portrayal within it.

On the one hand, this volume is permeated with allusions to Turkish culture, which establishes a fundamental sense of collective love of country. On the other hand, the allegiance to this foundation causes an inability to adapt to new surroundings and so rather engenders rigidity, which in turn cultivates frustration at being in limbo. Frustration is an emotion expressed equally as often as love of country in *Türken deutscher Sprache*. The collec-tive image of Turks, to judge from this anthology, is one that is still in a state of transition. In Chapter 6, it will become clear that the self-image has changed with the transition of one generation to another. In *Türken deutscher Sprache*, however, the standard situation of Turks in the process of becoming accustomed to the strangeness and novelty of Germany is unmistakable.

Of further interest in this collection of works by Turkish authors is the image of Germans as perceived by fellow Turks. With the exception of the above-mentioned story by Alev Tekinay, which conveys many positive impressions of Germany, their poems and short prose texts echo the unfinished work— acculturation—manifest in most contributions to the anthology. Indeed, the primary problem for the protagonists of Tekinay's story is their exaggerated and therefore blind acceptance of Germany; the reader comes to view this as the tragic flaw in the characters that will prove their undoing when they begin to view Germany more realistically. Utopia does not exist, Tekinay teaches the reader. As the narrator says, it is not that anyone who leaves the paradise of Germany is a fool (45), but rather he is a fool to view Germany as a paradise at all. Tekinay's logic is a standpoint from which other authors of *Türken deutscher Sprache* might well profit. She takes an uncomfortable but realistic posi-tion on the fence and defends the worthwhile aspects of both countries even as she points out their drawbacks.

Those authors who have not yet reached equilibrium in coming to terms with life in Germany tend more toward starkly negative imagery. Özür Savasçi takes the river Isar as a symbol for Germany—cold and inhospitable— in "An die Isar" (53). He speaks apologetically to the river and accuses it of being unfit to be the theme of a poem, and unfit as a means of escape or even suicide. The perceived or actual inhospitability of Germany and Germans is the foremost facet in the image conveyed, but a determination of the cause explains why the perception arose. Like America to millions of immigrants from Europe, Germany seemed to countless Turks to be a promised land of limitless opportunity. This paradisiacal view of Germany did not correspond to reality, and disillusionment followed. Senoçak laments the lack of this facet of the collective Turkish identity in the worker of "Du bist ein Arbeitsknochen" (89): rationality, clear-sightedness, and insight into the problem of presenting and defining oneself.

Senoçak's poem is a chronology of the foreign workers' recruitment, arrival, hopes, and disillusionment; impersonal occurrences and personal reactions are juxtaposed in a telling account. The worker of the poem still waits, perhaps to be accepted into German society, but apparently in vain, for he speaks of how waiting makes one old, but not necessarily happy. He allows himself to be used until he is used up and has no recourse but to leave Germany for a homeland that either no longer will acknowledge him as belonging there or in which he cannot feel at home (90). Senoçak demonstrates compassion, but the warning in his poem is clear: Because the worker would not or could not see the chain of events for what they were, namely, chains that soon locked him into an undesirable fate, he became the victim of his own lack of understanding. Senoçak's poem is in this sense an admonition to his coutrymen in Germany: As you present yourselves, so will you be perceived. This is the message of his text.

Exacerbating the disillusionment are the instances of bona fide xenophobia that Ihsan Atacan documents in "Begegnungen": a little Turkish boy sits all alone on a playground because the German children rejected him for not being like them (26).

Kemal Kurt's contribution to *Türken deutscher Sprache*, "Das Epos vom mustergültigen Ausländerle" (87), mockingly depicts the ideal foreigner, dubbed condescendingly 'the model little foreigner,' whose desirability lies in his being no trouble to the country that benefits from his work. Kurt vents his disgust at the mentality that views the recruited menial laborers as a burden and an eyesore in German society. Upon reading his poem, a picture can be drawn of the totally unrealistic expectations and of the selfish need not to be bothered by social needs within Germany. Ideally, foreigners should not desire a humane standard of living, but should merely dissolve into thin air between work shifts. The criticism is scathing, but it is not directed solely at Germans; the Turkish worker has been weak enough to succumb to materialism; he works for the superficial rewards of a video-recorder or a used car. Although the German attitude is made to appear more despicable, it is not the lone target of the poem. Criticism of both Germans and Turks is a motif that surfaces often, especially in poems of second-generation writers, as will be demonstrated in the chapter dealing with more recent aspects of Turkish writers' literature.

Of all the writers of Turkish descent in Germany today, the author who most assiduously portrays both Germans and Turks is one who does not even write in German: Aras Ören combines with subtlety and insight the complexities of Germans and Turks co-existing, changes perspectives to allow the reader to identify first with one and then the other, and finally leaves the ultimate insight to the perspicaciousness of the reader. Although a reader might deduce from his nationality that he would side strictly with Turks and depict the Germans as the bad guys, this is not the case. Ören's careful and precise eye detects the underlying humanity—both its good and its bad elements—in both nationalities. The comparison of his and other non-native German writers' depiction of modern German society with that of native German writers is stark in contrast. As Harald Weinrich states in the *Zeitschrift für Kulturaustausch,* contemporary German litera-ture conveys the impression that there are no foreigners in Ger-many, and hence no problems associated with them (14). (There are, of course, exceptions, such as Sten Nadolny's *Selim oder die Gabe der Rede,* which features a guru-like Turkish boxer and his German protogé.)

The literature by German-speaking Turks in Germany has no such gap—quite the opposite. Before returning to the image of Germans in the works of Turkish authors in the Federal Repub-lic, a brief overview of the image of Germany and Germans in native Turkish works will serve as an introduction and comparison. Wolfgang Riemann, in his examination of the Turkish image of Germany, *Das Deutschlandbild in der modernen türkischen Literatur*, takes a phrase from Turkish, *Almanya edibiyati* or *Almanya öyküleri*, meaning "Germany literature" or "Germany stories" to describe the primarily personal accounts of Turks who have lived in Germany (40). One of the writers recognized by Riemann as one of the founding fathers of this literature is the recent Adelbert von Chamisso Prize recipient Yüksel Pazarkaya. The beginning phase, according to Riemann, lasted from the late sixties to the early seventies and was characterized by the persona of the *Gastarbeiter*. This was followed by the second phase, dominated by the fates of those who remained in Turkey while a member of their family worked in Germany (42). A few works were also translated later into German, presumably to take advantage of the boom of the victims' literature or *Betroffenheits-literatur*. Also notable, and subsequently translated into German, is the collection of stories published by the established writer Fürüzan after she received a stipend from the DAAD, the German Academic Exchange Service, to come to Germany in 1975/76. She documented the situation of the foreign worker in Berlin, where she lived, and in the industrial region of Germany, the Ruhr Valley. The title of her work is telling: *Logis im Land der Reichen*. According to the editor of *Logis im Land der Reichen*, Rosemarie Kuper of dtv, Fürüzan (whose full name is Fürüzan Selçük) is the most recent in a line of Turks reporting from Germany on Germany since the era between the turn of the century and the onset of Hitler's rise to power (150). These works were the answer to the question: "How do the Turks see us Germans?" The main difference between her predecessors and herself, say the author and Kuper, lies in the different status of the Turk then and now. A travelogue writer from the privileged upper class in the early 1900s probably arrived at the opulent Frankfurt train station on the Orient Express, while his modern-day counterpart comes from rural Anatolia, and stands in line with countless countrymen and women at the airport, hoping, like thousands before them in one year alone, to receive work permits (51). Kuper indicates one vital difference beyond the socio-economic status that sets the modern-day Turks in Germany apart from their predecesssors: The Turks of the early twentieth century saw the Germans as friends and benefactors, the great models. As noted by Alev Tekinay in the February 1986 issue of the bilingual magazine *Bizim Almanca/Unser Deutsch*, the Turks had been allies of the Germans since the time of Wilhelm II (48). In honor of this friendship all Islamic prisoners of war were afforded special treatment in a special camp in Berlin/Wünsdorf, where the approximately four thousand inmates had their own mullah, according to a September 1987 article in *Bizim Almanca/Unser Deutsch* (16).

This image dissipated with Hitler, when Germans of the intellectual strata benefited from Turkey's offer of asylum. Fürüzan says the Turks are suffering betrayed friendship after the irresponsible way in which Germany recruited them. Kuper is quick to add that Fürüzan also critizes her own country's role in the fate of the *Gastarbeiter*, a note that is nearly inaudible in any other Turkish writer's depiction of Turks and Germans (152).

The Turks writing in German are an exception, although their criticism of the Turks is less vehement than that of the Germans. The Germans are depicted, to take a broad overview of all the Turkish writers' works, as a rather reserved folk, reserved to the point of lacking in emotions. Many writers associate this lack of human warmth with the German prosperity, *Wohlstand*, and see materialism as engendering dispassion. Taking this a step further, Kemal Kurt's poem in *Türken deutscher Sprache*, "Südafrika ist ein fernes Land" (230), is his pointed comparison between South Africa and Germany. In it he quotes from hearsay descriptions of South Africa in examples that hold true for Germany as well, from the lack of voting rights to the closed doors to certain races to language snobbism to corruption and deportation. There is a name for the system in South Africa, he says: *apartheid*. Kurt closes his poem by asking in feigned innocence why he should care about a distant country like South Africa. He is really pointing the finger at the indifference and ignorance, inhumanity and injustice, for which there is no one label but from which one cannot distance onself, and saying "charity begins at home."

Kurt's poem "'schuldigung" (226) also has a tone that cannot be classified as maudlin; it is sardonic, accusatory, and barely masks rage. It is the opposite of "Du bist ein Arbeitsknochen," Zafer Senoçak's poem: it takes the Germans to task for seeing Turks as undeserving of compassion. As with Senoçak's poem, language is a key element. Here, the carefully chosen, pedantic preciseness underscores the fact that most Germans are surprised if a Turk speaks passable German, and that in order to make an impression, state a grievance, or even share a mere observation, it must not be couched in less than perfect German. In addition, the elegant style calls the reader's attention to the perversity of beautiful language used to describe bare-bones existential needs and injustices regarding those needs. At the same time, flowery German is used as a gesture of reaching out, of appeal, of solidarity, of hope that the gesture will lead to understanding and tolerance. Kurt expresses hope, tenacity, and a sense of some forthcoming justice that Germans and Turks are to achieve together.

A year after the third anthology appeared from the dtv, the Institut für Ausländerbeziehungen, publisher of the previously mentioned *Zeitschrift für Kulturaustausch*, devoted that entire issue—subtitled "Aber die Fremde ist in mir"—to the experience of migration and the image of Germany in modern Turkish literature. Although the title did not make specific that most of the literature presented in the volume was by Turks in Germany, nonetheless it was. Other contributions included examinations of the image of Germany prevalent in Turkey and reprints of texts by various authors in the Federal Republic, including texts from *Türken deutscher Sprache*, among others.

A particularly extreme illustration of a negative image of Germans is to be found in the poems of Sadi Üçüncü, whose doctoral degree positions him outside the category of *Gastarbeiter*, but who feels nonetheless equally stricken by the attitudes he sees Germans exhibiting toward Turks. Üçüncü came to

Germany as an adult in the mid-seventies. Few of his poems appearing in the CIS-Verlag's *Freund gib mir deine Hand* address friendly advances on the part of Germans. More often, they express wrenchingly painful confrontation or pure rejection. Üçüncü may not be a *Gastarbeiter*, but he is used to being treated like one, to judge by his poem "Ich bin der Ausländer" (41).

Despite the overdone pathos marked by frequent repetition of the phrase "I am the foreigner the scum of the earth," it is clear what kind of image Üçüncü seeks to portray of Germans: unfeeling, xenophobic, racist. Üçüncü gives a reason for Germans' lack of compassion in the poem "Ein kaltes Land Deutschland" (44): Like many authors, he uses the German weather, with long winters and a dearth of sunshine, as a metaphor and actual reason for emotional coldness.

Authors who highlight the differences between Turks and Germans are, not surprisingly, ones who still feel very Turkish themselves. Any individuals who themselves are straddling the cultural fence between two nationalities will naturally not perceive the distinctions as drastically as those who are more strongly rooted in one culture or the other. In this sense, the disappearance of German-Turkish comparisons in works by second-generation authors is remarkable only because the preceding generation so emphasized the disparity.

Zehra Çirak's emphasis on universality is evident in her contribution to the *Zeitschrift für Kulturaustausch*, "Brief an meine Schwestern in meinen Heimaten" (145). When asked about the topic of this poem, whose title seems to indicate patriotism or at least to address her compatriots, Çirak hastens to point out that not only is the word *Schwestern* (sisters), plural, but so is the word for home country, *Heimaten*. She rejects the notion of one homeland as restrictive, choosing instead globality of belonging, and expressing it via the word "homes." She says that all the women of the world are her sisters, not exclusively in the feminist sense, but as co-inhabitants of this planet.

Despite the overwhelming sense of community that Turkish writers allude to as primary to Turkish culture, the sense of the collective will does not extend to the political arena in the works of Turkish writers in Germany. Aras Ören comes the closest to overt politicizing in his portrayals of the down-trodden worker. Not only is a lack of political involvement in Germany evident in most works, but even opinions on Turkey's political life are missing. Only Ören puts critical words regarding Turkish politics into the mouth of one of his characters, Kazim Akkaya, in "Was Will Niyazi in der Naunynstraß," who cites politics in Turkey as the reason for his coming to Germany (33).

The view of politics in Germany is limited to such immediacies as living and work permits; like the worker in Ören's texts, the Turks, as they are generally portrayed by fellow Turks, are hapless pawns in a game of power, be it capitalism or politics. The main political concern of Turks is summed up in Ihsan Atacan's previously mentioned "Begegnungen": An old man asks a young worker about the conditions in Germany when the latter returns to visit his village in Turkey (29).

The search for a voice to express an identity is inextricably linked to the search for stability among Turkish nationals, whether in their own or in a new country. As HSM in dtv's *In zwei Sprachen leben* expresses it, the Turks are straddling the cultural fence, sitting on two chairs at once. HSM postulates, however, that Turks are not at home in either language (14).

The Turkish writers in Germany today belie that statement: They are increasingly constructing for themselves a niche in a language that is not their own.

NOTES

1. Gino Chiellino, personal interview, 11 March 1985.

2. See articles on this matter in both June/July 87 and December/January 87/88 issues of *Die Brücke.*

3. Cf. personal interviews with Gino Chiellino, Franco Biondi, and Saliha Scheinhardt.

4. Zehra Çirak, personal interview, 18 January 1988.

5. Zehra Çirak, personal interview, 18 January 1988.

Chapter Five

Voice As Language:
"Hände lernen das deutsche ABC"

Yüksel Pazarkaya belongs to the first generation of writers who did not grow up speaking both German and Turkish, since they came to Germany as adults. He questions his own ability to write in German. He knowingly describes the feeling of trying to become a fish in German waters. He speaks of the dangers of this situation, of losing his identity as poet and writer, and preaches careful consideration. Since literature is language, argues Pazarkaya in the periodical *Lernen in Deutschland*, no one should undertake to write in it who is not also grounded in its cultural history (77).

If one accepts and follows Pazarkaya's reasoning to its logical conclusion, then none of the writers from Turkey, and especially those of the so-called first generation, have any right setting their hand to a manuscript in German. Are they fools or egotists, preposterous or vain? Are their efforts doomed, as Pazarkaya posits, to tragedy for their hubris, their casting to the winds of all self-esteem and deference for their craft? How can an author such as Saliha Scheinhardt make the absurd claim quoted in the August/September 1988 issue of *Die Brücke* that the Federal Republic is her spiritual and linguistic home? (57). A writer, says Pazarkaya, has to be capable of reflecting on his existence and identity, of preferring the inner torment to any appearance of satisfactory conquest. Only in this way can writers avoid tragedy and, in the process, prove their worth.

The inner torment, the trail of tears that Pazarkaya mentions, allows for a poetic bilingualism. In fact, the current state of the world often forces bilingualism upon us, especially on those whose lives are marked by emigration. Saliha Scheinhardt, Aysel

Özakin, Zehra Çirak and Yüksel Pazarkaya, to name a few, are vastly disparate in background vis-à-vis their German but are joined by a mutual intent: They all have decided on their primary language.

Despite the advantages of having chosen a language, other entanglements accompany the duality of daily life for Turkish-German writers, especially those who have grown up in the Federal Republic, as set out in Pazarkaya's article on Turks in Germany printed in the November 1985 issue of *Bizim Almanca/ Unser Deutsch*. He points to the difference between his experience and that of young Turkish people in Germany today, saying they have German as a primary language. He regrets that they do not write in German as well, but allows that it may be attributable to their lack of belonging in either country (41).

In the same periodical Nedim Gürsel, a Turkish writer living in France, speaks of the same topic, yet with a more positive prognosis, indicating that writers should develop their own individual language and style (40). Gürsel has articulated what is at the core of the issue of identity and language. For the most part, language and identity are taken to be inseparable, Siamese twins of the soul whose forced division results, at best, in neither ever being quite the same, and at worst, in the destruction of both. Although language is the primary tool by which identity is revealed, the two can be disengaged, as is apparent in the works of most of the Turkish authors: Even those who grew up in Germany are, as Gürsel points out, often equally at home or even equally alienated in both languages, but at the same time are involved in a process of identity-seeking that includes yet transcends linguistic boundaries. Since their first language was Turkish, their use of German as a literary language demonstrates their success in establishing an identity that is not hampered by its linguistic trappings. The use of German they have in common; their disposition toward it, however, varies.

Pazarkaya's contribution to the *Zeitschrift für Kulturaustausch*, "deutsche sprache" (144), expresses devotion to and appreciation of German. It opened for him the door to the thoughts of German-speaking geniuses, and more than that, gave him a second home. He defends the language, saying inability to speak in a language indicates a lack of idenity with it, and that German gives him the same hope as his mother tongue of Turkish.

In sharp opposition to the approbatory tone of Pazarkaya's poem is the quote in *Informationen Deutsch als Fremdsprache*, in which Sinasi Dikmen, well known for his satiric plays and short stories, states that for him, German is a weapon against Germans (274).

Pazarkaya and Dikmen are not as far apart in their attitudes toward German as they may first appear to be. Each seeks in the new language a means of coping with the society that speaks that language: Dikmen confronts the Germans directly with his satiric jabs, and Pazarkaya flees the coarser, more negative aspects of the society by turning to the sublime profundities of that society's finest minds. Still, unlike Kemal Kurt in the poem "an dem weltunatergang verdienen wir uns cumm und dämlich" from his volume *beim nächsten ton*, both seem to have found a comfortable working relationship with the language.

Despite his pessimistic tone, Kurt 's use of the language of another belies his poem's stated distaste for it. Rather than rejecting German outright, he seems to be asking instead how long it will feel alien to him. The border must be crossed into the realm of ease and familiarity within the language, just as the border into cultural parity must be crossed, not only by Turks becoming accustomed to Germany, but by Germans becoming accustomed to the Federal Republic's increasingly multicultural population. The fourth and final dtv anthology focuses on precisely that issue, as is reflected in its title *Über Grenzen*. Edited not by Irmgard Ackermann, but by Karl Esselborn—with a foreword by Ackermann—the anthology features already known authors such as Alev Tekinay, Zehra Çirak, Kemal Kurt, Sadi Üçüncü, Hasan Dewran, Hülya Özkan, Ertunç Barin, Ihsan Atacan and Osman Engin, as well as a few others whose contribution to *Über Grenzen* remains their sole publication.

A few contributions, such as Kurt's "Keine Vorkommnisse an der Grenzübergangstelle" (15-19)—a slightly surreal depiction of border regulations—deal with a border crossing, passports and regulations, while others focus on inner boundaries. Characteristic of the focus on inner borders is Zehra Çirak's poem "sich warm laufen" (220). She points out that it is coldest on bridges, using a bridge as a symbol for the inner limbo undergone during acculturation. With the exception of the first anthology, the last, *Über Grenzen*, contains the proportionately fewest contributions by Turkish authors. While this cannot be taken as indicative of an overall trend away from writing by Turks, combined with the fact that dtv has not published any other anthologies of this type it could indicate that the writers are not reliant on anthologies. Most prefer to take their chances alone rather than to be clustered under the rubric "Foreigners' Works" in an anthology.[1] When featured in an anthology, they are put on display as a novelty—foreigners actually writing in German—and the scrutiny of readers whose primary motivation is curiosity functions as a lens that distorts the writers' works. Having chosen to write in German, they prefer that readers take the element of language as a given rather than as an oddity.[2]

NOTES

1. Cf. personal interviews with Zehra Çirak, Kemal Kurt, and Gino Chiellino.

2. Zehra Çirak, personal interview, 2 June 1988.

3. See page 38.

Chapter Six

"German Language, Good Language..."?
"Deutsche Sprache, gute Sprache..."?

In her *Zeitschrift für Kulturaustausch* article "In der Fremde hat man eine dünne Haut.... Türkische Autoren der 'Zweiten Generation oder die Überwindung der Sprachlosigkeit," Irmgard Ackermann[1] credits second-generation writers with adopting German at their arrival during their formative years (28). It is true that most of the children of *Gastarbeiter* speak better German than Turkish. Ackermann goes on to say that what distinguishes the second-generation authors from the rest of their peers is that they are not silent (28). Ackermann, perhaps because of her work with first-generation writers, has fallen into what publishers and writers alike have come to view as a trap ever since the venue of literature by non-German speaking writers: She thrusts all writers into a mold of suffering. True, the *Gastarbeiterliteratur* and *Betroffenheitsliteratur* focused on the plight of Turks in Germany, but these facets of the literature were earlier, and more importantly, were written primarily by *Gastarbeiter* who were, in actuality, suffering the pangs of culture shock and undergoing the throes of integration. The writers of the second generation view themselves as at home in Germany, despite the remnants of hostility initially directed at their parents. They do not see themselves as *Gastarbeiter*, and hence do not see any need to address themselves to this issue, at least not as directly as their predecessors. For them, the issue is not whether they belong in Germany, but how to adjust to the fact of belonging.[2]

Their nerve center, to return to the issue of language and identity, is less which *language* is theirs, but which *identity*. They use the language they can utilize more fully, German, to grapple with reality. Zehra Çirak's early poem "nicken mit dem kopf

heißt nein" shows one individual's development away from the
Turkish family to a stubborn self-sufficiency and self-definition.
The title is a reference to cultural differences; in some non-
European cultures in Africa and Asia, a nod is actually a gesture
of negation or denial. Çirak's persona deliberately uses this
gesture to delude her family into thinking she is in agreement,
while inwardly she is setting up new constructs and rules of
behavior in preparation for rebellion against the injustice and
otherness her family represents for her.

The young Turkish girl of the poem above rails against the
oppressive upbringing she receives at the hands of her conserva-
tive, probably orthodox, Islamic parents because she sees the
need to be like her counterparts in the native-German milieu. So
too does a young man, Zafer Senoçak, stretch out past the boundaries of separate German and Turkish worlds in his contribution to *Türken deutscher Sprache*, "Ohne Grenzen" (245).

Senoçak's poem addresses the universality of life, and this
disposition aligns him with Çirak in "Brief an meine Schwestern
in meinen Heimaten"; both demonstrate that commonality
rather than diversity be the focus. Senoçak's other poem relating
to the topic of borders, "Doppelmann," mentioned in Chapter 3,
which also appeared in the *Zeitschrift für Kulturaustausch*, does
just the opposite: In it, Senoçak reveals the divisiveness that
biliguality can engender in the speaker of two culturally and
linguistically disparate languages.

In choosing the German language over their native Turkish,
the writers demonstrate their willingness, even eagerness, to be
a part of the German-speaking community and to take part in
the country's discourse. This is an inherently political gesture.
As Gino Chiellino expressed (to general approval on the part of
the multi-national participants, of whom nearly two-thirds were
Turks) at the conference sponsored by the Evangelische
Akademie on "Literature in a Multi-Cultural Context," the intent
behind a foreigner's writing in another language is to re-order
the semantic codes within that language and to give it new life.
He expressed as his personal goal the politicizing of the German
language toward a new semiotics, for example away from Nazi

rhetoric, in which *Heimat* or home, a word often thematicized by foreign writers, had a negatively nationalistic ring to it.

Levent Aktoprak, a young Turk residing in Munich, who came to Germany, like Çirak, at a very young age, confronts the topic of language as it relates to racist or facist tendencies in his contribution to the *Zeitschrift für Kulturaustausch*, "Entwicklung" (143). His persona begins by learning the German ABCs only to use it to read German graffitti, such as "Foreigners Go Home." The poem closes with an ironic statement, quoting the question on the narrator's high school baccalaureate exam: What were the causes of German fascism?

Aktoprak is seeking to accomplish the forefronting of the cultural skeletons in the German closet, while Chiellino exposes the German linguistic skeleton. As writers, both turn to the medium in which the skeletons are clothed to unmask them as racist and counterprogressive.

But the approach taken by Chiellino and Aktoprak is merely one way in which non-natives transform the German language. Written texts are very effective in accomplishing this task, because there is no interference on the level of accent. Many of the Turks who came to Germany while no longer children find that their residual accents form a barrier to communication at times: The native German who hears pidgin German is often likely to conclude that the speaker is uneducated and even unintelligent, although this is rarely the case; similarly, some Germans' reaction to an accent is guardedness, a lack of openness. This reserve could constitute an impediment to the aim of imbuing the language with new meanings. Kemal Kurt's "'schuldigung"[3] illustrates how facility in German is still not considered a given; the poem plays upon the surprise elicited when refined German is heard coming from a Turk.

The segregating function of language is illustrated by the following two texts. The first is a sign described in "Sie haben mich zu einem Ausländer gemacht." Seen in a bar in Germany, it mocks the pidgin German—*Tarzandeutsch*—of infinitives and faulty syntax spoken by some foreigners and many native Germans trying to communicate with foreigners (150).

The belittling intent of the lines is obvious. By aping the broken German of foreigners without a firm grasp of German, the native emphasizes his own superiority and refusal to demonstrate any approval for the non-native's attempt at speaking the target langauge.

A similar form of German is exibited in "tarzanca": *Tarzandeutsch* is called "Tarzanese" in Turkish and is the title of an unpublished manuscript by Zehra Çirak, who chooses to use pidgin German to express the commiseration for the situation of Turks whose meager German skills are but one cause of distress. The origins of their unhappiness and stress lie in the conditions imposed upon foreigners by German society. Ironically, they converse with one another in German. The choice of German adds a poignancy that borders on hopelessness. They speak German in the hopes of being accepted in the new land, but their attempts are not only futile, as their situation indicates, but sadly, they are also inadequate. Speaking pidgin German relegates them in German society to laughing stocks and scapegoats, since flawed German is generally equated with flawed intelligence and hence diminished worth by the German listener. Writing her poem in German, however, she puts the scene before German readers, forcing them to look beyond the syntax and accent to the content, to see the humanity, the emotions of the speakers, and most of all to recognize the common frailities. The "no," which is never spoken out loud but always sotto voce, is an expression of dissatisfaction with which everyone can identify; the child wishing to stand up to his parents, or the discontented citizen grumbling about bureacracy who is too timid or too sure of the futility of protest to speak louder.

The characteristic lack of pathos in Çirak's works is evident in the above poem as well: while writers such as Üçüncü attempt to garner the reader's sympathy by emphasizing the emotional element, Çirak prefers to let the poem stand or fall on its own merit, and not to overtly influence the reader's reaction. Frequently, she highlights the prosaic to the point of comedy, as is the case in the previous poem. The poem's "Tarzan German" *is* comical, and this comic relief allows readers to distance themselves from the poem. Rather than dismissing the poem as too intense to be bearable, the slight touch of humor instead causes readers to want to linger with its content. Çirak may well have discovered a key element that will allow her literature to not only develop beyond a misère, but also to reach a readership jaded from an overdose of literature on suffering. She writes solely in German, saying that language accords her the flexibility necessary for her well-turned phrases. The title of one of her poems, "deutsche sprach gute sprache," is apt in this context; contortions of syntax and semantics to which German seems particularly suited are like tantalizingly valuable tools to a language smith. In the realm of humor and satire such linguistic twistings are useful; as Çirak points out, they serve them well. Successful humor relies in large measure on an escalation of anticipatory hypotheses by the listener or reader by building on sets of standard possibilities inherent in the frame of reference of the listener, usually by combining words and phrases in recognizable patterns that conjure up images or moods. In this poem, Çirak builds on the idiomatic phrase *"deutsche Sprache, schwere Sprache"* jestingly used by those seeking to justify mistakes or confusion in using German. Çirak exchanges difficult (*schwer*) for good (*gut*), and leads the reader to expect just the opposite of mistakes or confusion. Instead, the level of difficulty is drasti- cally escalated, to the point that even natives are hopelessly lost in the grammatical labyrinth and can disentangle themselves only by undertaking a second, slow reading and painstakingly mapping out exactly who is subject and object. Once at the end of the poem, the reader finds it is very humorous indeed being caught in the trap of expecting ease yet encountering severely confusing difficulties that substantiate the original idiom that set up the level of expectation in the first place.

Humor in the texts written by Çirak demonstrates not only her command of the language's complexities, but her healthy scepticism of it as well. Her down-to-earth approach to life is reflected in her literary efforts, for which she was awarded the Adelbert von Chamisso Fellowship in 1989 and the Hölderlin Förderpreis in 1993. Her most humorous poems are tongue-in-cheek, as if she were saying to herself and the reader not to be so self-important, not to take language at its face value: This very quality of displacement within language makes up the essence of the value of Çirak's work. Her work is refreshing and will certainly continue to excite interest and praise in the future. As Albert von Schirnding puts it in the *Süddeutscher Zeitung* of February 27, 1989, she possesses unmistakable individuality.

A friend and compatriot of Çirak is Kemal Kurt, whose early works include autobiographical vignettes of his childhood, rather predictably titled *Bilder einer Kindheit*, as well as poems in the dtv anthologies and the aforementioned volume of poems whose title aligns it perfectly with the theme of voice: *Beim nächsten Ton*. Kurt speaks English as well as Turkish and German, as a result of having studied engineering in Florida, and in the past has even translated other Turkish authors' works from German into Turkish to be read to a Turkish-speaking audience. His mastery of languages is apparent in his latest poems, several of which play with expectation and language in the way just described of Çirak. In the middle of an erotic love poem, within a cycle titled *das gegenteil von poesie*—Kurt's definition in this volume of the emotion called love—Kurt's persona speaks words of love: "I like you" (*ich habe dich gern*) and follows the statement with a sudden twist on the sentiment "*du kannst mich auch gern haben*," meaning literally "you can like me too," but in slang usage meaning approximately, "well, same to you, bub" (18). The reader is jolted into wondering who is voicing these words, the lover or the beloved, and why the sudden change in feeling? While this is not purely humorous, its wry overtones have perhaps the same source as the distancing effect that allows Kurt the sardonic self-portrait he offers early in the volume. The title of one poem indicates a subtle distancing effect: A grammatical error in the words "howl with them wolves" (*mit die wölfen heulen*) attracts the readers' attention in a way that the more obviously humorous poem preceding it does not, since the humorous poem is headed by the same title without the error in grammar: "*mit den wölfen heulen*" (howl with the wolves) (40).

Howling with the wolves, that is, running with the pack, is a concept that Kurt is testing, tasting on his tongue, as it were, for the potential flavor or bad aftertaste; seeing if it is to his liking, and, judging by the final word, *heulsusen*—which is German for *crybabies*—it does not agree with him and he rejects the idea.

Just as Kemal Kurt utilizes wryness to distance himself in his poems, so too does Sinasi Dikmen in his cabarets, but the difference lies in the target and in the effect. Kurt expresses superiority, a sense of rising above the pack, while Dikmen, whose satirical cabaret pieces are known and enjoyed throughout the Federal Republic, pokes fun at himself and his target. He points a mocking finger at stereotypes and prejudices, as the title of his book, *Wir werden das Knoblauchkind schon schaukeln* , makes clear. The image of Turks as a nation of smelly garlic eaters is but one stereotype Dikmen ridicules. In the one-sided dialogues contained in the book, Dikmen speaks to an imaginary countryman, a yokel who has no idea of what life in Germany means. Dikmen speaks to the naïve listener in a condescending, instructive tone, and he jeers not only at the image Germans have of the Turk as a hick but also at his fellow Turks, whose naïveté makes them the butt of jokes, and he even does not spare himself (18). Other passages from *Wir werden das Knoblauchkind schon schaukeln* address the topic of discontent due to, and protest of, injustice toward Turks in Germany. Nonetheless, tones of German arrogance echo throughout Dikmen's statements, as if the Turkish speaker had internalized the reproaches directed against him.

Another satirist, Osman Engin, whose "Türkischer Brumm-schädel" appeared in dtv's *Über Grenzen* (100-102), also depicts the Turkish protagonist as having internalized the "normalcy" of a Turk's life in Germany. He dreams that all of Germany's sole aim is to honor and repay the Turks. The reader does not realize it is a dream until the word *Klingelingeling*—the ring of an alarm clock—appears. The mood following the alarm allows the intensity of the satire to have its full effect. The dreamer is glad the nightmare is over and that daily life can resume.

Unlike written texts, cabarets can employ a further element to underscore the humor or irony: On stage, Dikmen, a first-generation immigrant who came to Germany as an adult, exploits his thick Turkish accent and role as rural dolt in an urban setting to the embarassed delight of both Turkish and German audiences. In playing the fool, Dikmen can ingenuously address controversial topics such as the acquisition of German citizenship by Turks, housing shortages, and even racism. His first production, "Putsch in Bonn" (Coup in Bonn), was about the latent fears of Germans that Turks could overrun the country and dealt with issues in the mind of the nation as a whole, while the production of his *Knobi-Bonbon* cabaret *Vorsicht, Frisch Integriert*—about which he spoke in the February 1989 issue of *Bizim Almanca* (39)—focuses on the attempts of a Turkish man to deny his heritage in order to fit better into German society, which looks down on anything smacking of Turks. He is constantly tutoring his protegé, played by the other member of *Knobi-Bonbon*, Mehmet Omurca, in how to successfully Germanize himself even while he himself is learning Goethe by heart and practicing his best Teutonic mannerisms to convince the officials he deserves a German passport. Once he receives the passport from the hands of a brutally Prussian stuffed shirt of a bureaucrat (played also by Dikmen), he becomes fairly insufferable trying to be quintessentially German (forgetting the dislike he felt for certain German traits when he first came). Now the focus and the bane of his existence is his name, which his protegé still cannot pronounce "correctly"—that is, with a German pronunciation rather than the equally stressed Turkish pronunciation—a sign of his recalcitrance, Dikmen thinks. The protegé is, of course, the sensible one of the two; the audience is kept in stitches over Dikmen's overdone attempts at integration, for he sees only the outward trappings.

The interesting difference in Dikmen's cabaret is its consistent criticism of both Germans and Turks; in his satirical plays, Dikmen points out the universal nature of human flaws, and in doing so is admonishing his audience to see common traits instead of distinctions. His character's inability to differentiate is the actual target of his satire. It is Dikmen's method of showing the fallacy of stereotyping and overgeneralizing. In taking the Turks' and Germans' inner prejudices towards one another, and their secret images of themselves to the extreme, he can reveal the distortions inherent within them without appearing to offend either side directly and precipitate the mutual rapprochement. Dikmen sees his goal as a mutual rapprochement between Germans and Turks, a lessening of the hostilities (41). He names as the main reason for hostility the lack of understanding on the part of most of German society (41). Mutual acceptance and tolerance of both cultures is the goal of the two men.

The reason for the cabaret's name—*Knobi* being a slang abbreviation for garlic, a stereotypical symbol for Turks—comes from the tendency of Germans, according to Dikmen, to see Turks as virtual moustachioed garlic-bulbs. Dikmen's cabaret seeks to enlighten the German public in a manner much more immediate than books or even poetry readings can do, since the audience reacts on the spot (41).

The cabaret, although seen by Dikmen as a German phenomenon, takes on a Turkish aura as well; it bears the impression of Dikmen's and Omurca's native Punch-and-Judy act, Hacivat and Karagöz, a shadow play of very old origins. Not only are there merely two main characters, as in Karagöz, but these two are as often foe as friend and in their diverse personalities set one another off, representing two sides of an issue much as the Turkish shadow-play figures have always done. Dikmen views this juxtaposition as integrating a Turkish interpretation into the German language (41).

The sole criticism that can be leveled at Dikmen is his portrayal of women; to judge by his cabaret, *Gastarbeiter* are men. Indeed, the most attention given the female population of guest workers is their depiction as two-dimensional figures on the backdrop for a scene at the Foreigners' Agency (*Ausländerbehörde*). For all his carefulness about discrimination between cultures, Dikmen has left a gaping hole where discrimination toward women, in his own and in Germany's culture, could be portrayed.

NOTES

1. Irmgard Ackermann is the editor of *In Zwei Sprachen Leben*, *Als Fremder In Deutschland* and *Türken deutscher Sprache*.

2. Zehra Çirak, personal interview, 18 January 1988.

3. See page 38.

Chapter Seven

Women's Voice:
"Und die Frauen weinten Blut..."

A short excursion into Turkish culture is worthwhile in order to understand the portrayal of women in the literature of German-speaking Turkish writers. Andrea Baumgartner-Karabak and Gisela Landesberger cite the reforms sought by Kemal Atatürk at the beginning of this century as important in the Westerniza-tion of Turkish culture in their book *Die verkauften Bräute*; in 1930, women were granted suffrage in municipal elections, in 1931 polygamy was abolished and elementary education was made mandatory for both sexes, and in 1934 women were permitted to vote in parliamentary elections as well, which led in the same year to seventeen female Parliamentarians being elected to the governing body of an Oriental state (13). Yet, as Baumgartner-Karabak and Landesberger note, these reforms, while fairly successful in urban settings, went virtually un-heeded in rural communities because they were not based on a change in society's structure of near-feudalism, wherein the woman was the slave of her closest male family member (13). The Anatolian farmer remained untouched by government except in its function as policeman or tax collector. The isolation from government is not surprising even today, when one real-izes that villages are geographically and socially insular; since distance and weather do not permit easy travel from one village to another, the relationships within the village "clan" become central.

The sociologist Dr. Serim Timur concisely outlines the over-all structures of Turkish society in her contribution to Nermin Abadan-Unat's collection of essays *Die Frau in der türkischen Gesellschaft*, published by a Turkish-owned house, Dagyeli of

Frankfurt (55). In the essay on social structures, "Charakteristika der Familienstruktur in der Türkei," she points out that, contrary to common Western belief, patriarchal family units constitute only one-fourth to one-fifth of villages and small towns, a pattern that remains constant country-wide (62).

But, although not strictly patriarchally ruled, families in Turkey nonetheless still adhere to the custom of a bridegroom being chosen for a young girl, who herself has virtually no say in the matter. Two-thirds of the young women in the study reported their parents' choosing a spouse; one-half of the young men in the study reported the same. Marriage is perceived as an alliance between two families rather than merely an arrangement between two persons (70). And in areas beyond nuptial arrangements, the majority of households in the study reported that the husband had the deciding word over wife's, in-laws' or other family members' opinions (71). The basis for the predominantly male-oriented decision-making order is the Koran. Baumgartner-Karabak and Landesberger quote pertinent passages from the Koran as illustrations.

The essay "Die Auswirkungen der internationalen Arbeitsemigration auf die Rolle der Frau am Beispiel der Türkei," written by the editor, political scientist Dr. Abadan-Unat herself, deals with the effects that international migrant work has had on the role of women in Turkey. Contrary to common opinion, writes Dr. Abadan-Unat, a significant proportion of women exists in the work force of foreigners in Western Europe: In 1978 approximately 215,000 Turkish women were working in Europe, with 134,342 of them in West Germany (207). Dr. Abadan-Unat puts them into three categories: a female with a male head of household, a female enabling a man to emigrate by being forced to accompany him, and an autonomous woman emigrating by her own choice and alone (209).

She also lists other characteristics of female migrants: They are relatively young—more than half are between 25 and 30. More than a third are married, and most have children. Their education can be divided into two categories: More women than men have never gone to school (10% versus 7%); but more women than men who do have schooling have gone on to vocational or higher schools (38% versus 21%) (210). On the whole, women are not as frequently trained for a specific career, and the majority work in unskilled positions. A corollary to this factor is the statement by 55 percent of the women studied that their reason for coming to Germany was to keep the family together, not to work. The Turkish *Gastarbeiterin* also receives lower wages than her male counterpart; an average of between five and eight hundred marks as opposed to between nine hundred and one thousand five hundred for men (211).

The change and hence lack of stability in the structure of the family unit is one notable element (221). Compounding this difficulty is the problem of leaving some family members in Turkey until such time as they can be brought to Germany.

One integral element in the lack of stability and permanence is the question of authority. The woman left in Turkey to care for the children is more independent than if her husband were there; similarly, the Turkish woman in Germany who works to help support herself, her husband, and their children is not limited in her day-to-day existence as is the woman who does not work. In addition, she is exposed to new insights about education, training, and family planning. Still, as Dr. Abadan-Unat notes, the loosening of role definition is not as pervasive as might be assumed; traditions are upheld through such socialization factors as Koran schools, cultural programs, films and certain organs of the press, including movies (227).

Those most disadvantaged, in that they were those receiving the least consideration in the family unit of Turkish workers, were the marriageable daughters (227). Often young women are burdened with the care of their siblings and are forced to take on the role of substitute mothers, since the real mother is usually at work and therefore frequently absent.

Abadan-Unat also documents the psychological effects upon *Gastarbeiterinnen*—insecurity, feelings of discontinuity, relaxation of social controls, psychosomatic illness—and concludes that female workers cope less well with the various aspects of their new surroundings than do their male counterparts (236).

She infers that migration does not lead to the logical outcome of the emancipation of women (she defines emancipation as liberation from social pressures that hinder individual development and self-actualization), since emancipation requires reorganization of roles and division of work regarding family and free time (237). On the whole, then, Turkish women in Germany are not independent and not self-sufficient, though they certainly may wish to be.

Gaby Franger, the editor of the collection of interviews with Turkish Gastarbeiterinnen, *Wir haben es uns anders vorgestellt*, writes in her essay "Frauen aus der Türkei—zwischen Emanzipation und Unterdrückung" that these women are suffering from culture shock, and worse yet, that their position in the family is weakened unless they work outside the home, since as a housewife they are cut off and dependent upon their husbands for contact to their surroundings (95). Unlike Abadan-Unat, Franger says that emigration puts previously unknown limits on women, since now, in a foreign country whose customs are alien to them, the husbands worry about protecting their wives' honor. At the same time, says Franger, the nuclear family ties are intensified; the members of the immediate family are more socially reliant upon one another (97).

Yet the flipside of this situation, and a facet of Turkish women's lives not touched upon by Abadan-Unat, is the role of wife as primary breadwinner. West German industries concentrated much of their recruiting effort on women and, as a result, many came to Germany before their husbands, although as Baumgartner-Karabak and Landesberger discovered in their study, the decision to work in Germany was usually made for them by their husbands (72).

When a woman is recruited to work, and her husband and family come to Germany only after she has begun work and established residency, the woman is the finanacial head of the family; the spouse becomes a "househusband." Such an activity, says Franger, would have been unthinkable in the village, where social controls prohibit a man from undertaking such a "female" responsibility (99). The resultant conflicts often lead to divorce, but a Turkish woman experiences more difficulties than does her German peer in the case of a divorce, since in some cases, residence or work permits are often given to a wife only because her husband is a *Gastarbeiter*. Her living permit is often dependent on that of her husband; thus, divorce is nearly unthinkable out of fear of deportation (99).

The *soziale Netz*, the network of social programs designed to further the quality of life in Germany, is open to foreigners through their employers, unless they are employed illegally, but rarely does the wife of a *Gastarbeiter* take advantage of, for instance, a *Müttergenesungsheim* where women may go to recuperate from the day-to-day stress of being housewife, mother, and worker. The primary reason is that many workers who plan to return to Turkey count on claiming unused funds as cash when they leave Germany in order to buy into Turkish pension funds. A secondary reason is lack of information: Usually the system of socialized medicine provides for a *Kur*, and therefore the pension fund is not tapped. Franger blames the sheer number of regulations, and their opacity, for the misconceptions that prohibit many workers from exploiting the social services that are their due as workers (100).

The desire for self-sufficiency brings with it a range of problems that a German woman does not face: A Turkish woman who claims welfare for longer than half a year faces deportation (100), yet away from her rural home, a woman with children cannot easily seek employment that would enable her to support herself without the assistance she would have had from fellow villagers to care for her children. A younger, unencumbered woman whose standards have been colored by the German culture she has grown up in may seek to marry a man she knows and loves. If she is underage, however, there is no recourse for her if she wishes to defy her parents, except for the occasional halfway house where no real legal protection is offered short of suing the parents, something that occurs extremely rarely. Like Abadan-Unat, Franger also sees the young women as the most disadvantaged of all. There are exceptions—well-educated women from the big cities of Turkey who are able to assert themselves—but they are rare.

In the foreword to *Die Verkauften Bräute*, Susanne v. Paczensky notes exceptions such as Sevim Çelebi, parlamentarian in the Alternative Liste or Berlin Green Party (7), but the broad majority of Turkish women in the Federal Republic are either *Gastarbeiterinnen* or the wives of *Gastarbeiter* from rural Turkey. Their situation has been documented in the German press and in films; both media have concentrated on the position of the Turkish woman in her own male-dominated culture and in the world of the German culture. Although Jeanne Meerapfel's 1984 film *Die Kümmeltürkin geht* documents the true story of a single Turkish woman, whose insightful soul-searching after more than ten years as a seamstress in Germany leads her to the conclusion that she will never find happiness there, that she needs to return to Turkey, highlights the self-reliance and intelligence of the main figure, more widely viewed and acclaimed films such as Tevik Baser's *40 m^2 Deutschland* and Hark Bohm's *Yasmin* depict the main figure's unhappiness over being made captive by the male head of the household, ostensibly in order to protect her from the evils of the immorally free German society. Therefore, the predominant stereotype of the Turkish woman is that of a victim. Germans, for whom the socio-cultural system of Turkish male and female roles is close to incomprehensible, cannot see beyond the image of the harem as a symbol for Turkish norms; yet modern Turks, while not denying that image, insist that below the surface, it is the women, not the men, who rule. Be that as it may, the portrayal of women is complex and not completely free from frequently damaging stereotyping on the part of Turkish women writers themselves. Even a male writer such as Aras Ören portrays his women as victims of society who nonetheless have an amazing strength of will that enables them to survive, a trait that is reminiscent of Brechtian heroines.

As a backdrop to the portrayal of women in the literature of Turks in Germany, a brief overview of the depiction of Turkish women in the literature of their homeland is of interest. Although Abadan-Unat notes that her description of the place of women in Turkish literature is a mere overview, it is nonetheless useful to examine it (328). She concentrates on the narrative, that is novels and stories, although poetry also depicts women. As she points out, the woman is generally portrayed as the beloved and as the slave of the man, especially in the early Divan works (329). Later, a more realistic trend occurred in the late nineteenth century, only to be supplanted by a sentimental vision of love at the turn of the century. Much later, in the 1940s, the emphasis was placed on every-day people, but the woman remained the beloved (330). The main novelty in the following decades was the introduction, actually the societal permission regarding, eroticism (331). Thus, Abadan-Unat points out, despite change and different perspectives mirroring political and societal nuances, the image of women revolved primarily around the traditional roles of women. Even modern authors such as Fakir Baykurt choose to portray women as mothers, albeit mothers with strong universally human traits (339). This is true of the depiction of rural women; the urban Turkish woman is primarily a figure from the pen of writers who themselves are women. These figures, like their authors, fight for their rights as women and as persons (340). One woman writer already mentioned, Füruzan, depicts women in their struggle for survival, especially women from reduced circumstances such as poor mothers or prostitutes (342).

Three women writers who are contemporaries or near-contemporaries of Füruzan dominated the literary scene of Turkish authors in the Federal Republic until quite recently: Saliha Scheinhardt, Aysel Özakin, and Zehra Çirak. Of the three, Saliha Scheinhardt's prose works align her most with the subgenre of *Betroffenheitsliteratur*, and classify her, together with the film medium, as a conveyer of the image of Turkish women as sufferers. This does integration an injustice; it furthers the already stereotyped picture many in Germany have of Turkish women and may promote additional prejudices. In showing that modern Turkish women are not always victims, the vicious cycle could be broken. Fatma Arig, a journalist writing for the bilingual periodical *Bizim Almanca*, substantiates the criticism leveled at Scheinhardt. She declares that not only are German stereotypes fostered, but that the labels given Turks mark their own perception of themselves as well (19).

The pathos of Saliha Scheinhardt's stories, despite their established allure for German audiences, does the women whose lives she has documented in the form of semi-fictionalized stories no favors. Inevitably, the discussion following readings given by Scheinhardt revolves around such issues as the inequality of the sexes in Turkey or around the telling of highly personal anecdotes on personal relations that completely ignore any literary aspects of her books. A television interview and documentary about Scheinhardt, undertaken by one of Germany's three main networks in November of 1987, committed the same offense and offered the viewer nothing about the books of Saliha Scheinhardt; it instead offered an hour-long facsimile of "This is Your Life, Saliha Scheinhardt," in which the viewer watched the author revisit places she had lived and people she had known. Although she seems content with how she is presented, probably because the exotic element of her colorful life attracts readers, Scheinhardt, the holder of a Ph.D. in pedagogy, emphasizes the anecdotal over the literary. The majority of her novels, though ostensibly drawn from personal experience, perpetuate a view of Turkish women that is neither realistic nor helpful: The Turkish equivalent of hillbillies, the rural inhabitants of undeveloped villages in Eastern Turkey's Anatolia, are the face of Turkey most readily evident to the German to whose country they came as recruited workers in the last decades, and these are the people whom Scheinhardt has chosen to portray in her documentary novels. In an interview published in the August/September 1988 issue of the periodical *Die Brücke*, she said how glad she was to be able to speak for her compatriots (57). She almost flippantly protests the lack of awareness demonstrated by the average German about her native land (11). But her attempt at enlightening the German reading public takes them scarcely any further, since it focuses on the aspects of Turks already well known. Success has certainly been hers; she was the first Turkish woman in the Federal Republic to be named a writer in residence—*Stadtschreiberin*. The city of Offenbach near Frankfurt accorded her this honor, which—with 44,000 marks—is one of the highest in all of Germany, in 1985. Scheinhardt has been known to take a different tack and turn her gaze to other, more universal topics such as love; her book *Von der Erde bis zum Himmel Liebe*, published in 1988 by Büchergilde Gutenberg is a semi-fictitious rendering of the life of a persecuted Italian intellectual, Cesare, and is her first novel not to feature a Turkish woman. Other works focused primarily on the fate of Turkish women: *Frauen, die sterben, ohne daß sie gelebt hätten*; *Drei Zypressen*; *Und die Frauen weinten Blut*, published by EXpress Edition, Berlin in 1983, 1984 and 1985 respectively and *Träne für Träne werde ich heimzahlen*, which appeared in the *rowohlt aktuell* series in 1987. The latter is autobiographical, although it is fictionalized fact like all her semi-documentary works. (The titles of the first two are direct translations of cliché-like sayings from Turkish, *yaymadan ölenler* and *kan aglamak*.)

Scheinhardt is very passionate about her work and views it as a mission. She views her intensely emotional works as necessary not only to enlighten the Germans regarding the situation of Turks, but also to grant them an effective release not as inherent to the German psyche as to the Turkish one. She views the element of stong emotions as fundamental in the appeal her works have for German audiences, to which her high sales records testify.

Scheinhardt seems impervious to the potential her works have for perpetrating negative stereotypes about Turks in general and Turkish women in particular. Her first book, *Frauen, die sterben, ohne daß sie gelebt hätten*, begins with a pensive excursus about how readers react to negatively slanted newspaper articles on foreigners. While Scheinhardt's books do not contain perjorative perspectives or lies about her people, still she misses an opportunity to bring to her (almost exclusively German) readers a view different than the common one of Turks as underdogs. Her goal is enlightenment, but whether she achieves it by underscoring an already one-sided image of Turks is questionable. In the foreword, she continues her soliloquy by musing on the essence of prejudice (5).

Although Saliha Scheinhardt's crusade against injustice, undertaken after being counselor and friend to Suna, the woman driven to murder by her unhappy circumstances, is undeniably well-intentioned and even commendable, the fact that her books are such bestsellers logically means that the image of Turks as victims and sufferers is becoming even more widespread than the already popularly disseminated opinion of foreigners, especially foreign women, as ne'er-do-wells. With the publication of her new book, it is to be hoped that Scheinhardt is taking a new course that will allow her readers first to concentrate on the literary over the anecdotal, and second to overcome, even as the author herself seems to be doing, the focus on foreign women's misére. Scheinhardt has expressed a wish to be viewed as an author first and a foreigner second; but her works, with the exception of *Von der Erde bis zum Himmel Liebe*, permit the reader scarcely any other recourse than to do just the opposite.

For the reader satiated by Scheinhardt's rather heavy-handed message about minority women, the advent of *Von der Erde bis zum Himmel Liebe* was a welcome change. Scheinhardt does not stray far from her tried and true path, however; her steadfastness in bringing injustice to the German reading public's attention is commendable. However, the cynical reader will not be able to stifle a feeling that perhaps the popularity of this theme is in part the reason for Scheinhardt's singlemindedness.

As in her previous works, Scheinhardt chooses in *Von der Erde bis zum Himmel Liebe* to fictionalize actual historical events, as the dustcover summary of the book points out lest this fact escape a less astute reader. In this most recent work, the focus is not on a woman, but on Cesare, a young leftist intellectual man persecuted and eventually killed by the regime of his (unspecified) country. Though it is actually his brother who is sought, an earlier lie about who is the elder of the two becomes Cesare's undoing, since the torturers have merely been instructed to eliminate the elder—the brain behind the dissentionist press the two run—and to intimidate the younger.

While the plot captures the reader's interest consistently throughout the 187-page volume, not all the devices Scheinhardt utilizes are completely fortuitous. She has apparently abandoned the somewhat-limited, strictly autobiographical mode in favor of a multi-perspectival approach, in which first Cesare's love letters in italics to his future wife present the background information leading up to the years before their marriage, followed by the brother's soliloquy relating the events immediately before and during the arrest that led to Cesare's death. Following that section, titled "Bruderherz" (Brotherheart) (65-96), the wife's private thoughts overlap with and synthesize the two preceding chapters in "Zieh deine Augenbrauen nie zusammen" (Never Knit Your Brow) (97-154). This title is also a direct translation from Turkish: *kaslrini çatma.*

The emphasis on revealing injustice is as prevalent here as in Scheinhardt's earlier works, but the change in perspective has alleviated much of the pathos that threatened at times to alienate the reader wishing to arrive independently at conclusions regarding right and wrong. Scheinhardt's style has mellowed and improved with time. There is, however, some awkwardness to the stylistic devices in this novel; in stretching her literary muscles, Saliha Scheinhardt has occasionally exhausted her ability for skilled writing. One example is the strain that the reader feels in trying to accept as natural the brother's soliloquy. "Bruderherz" is written as if he were addressing the departed Cesare, yet why should he tell the deceased in such detail about events that both experienced together? It is painfully obvious that the sole reason is to inform the reader; this glaring flaw in the narrative line mars the quality of the novel.

The primary device Scheinhardt uses in all sections of *Von der Erde bis zum Himmel Liebe* is that of apostrophe. Each person who has had a relationship with Cesare evokes his presence, the spirit in which he lived his life, by speaking to him as if he still lived. Indeed, for all of the speakers, Cesare is not dead. His resurrection in spirit is due less to their inability to accept the fact of his death (although especially his wife goes through a period of denial) than to the enduring nature of his personality. Cesare lives on after his own actual death in their memories of him and in the manner in which he has made an impact on their lives. Two elements of the work, however, are less than credible and thereby detract from the effectiveness of apostrophe in this setting: The reader is never convinced that Cesare's wife, a self-sufficient modern women with an enlightened sense of equality and a well-developed self-esteem, should quite rapidly turn into a woman content to submit to the whims of a fairly stubborn and conventionally male sense of propriety and ownership within a marriage. Maria's declarations of love are genuine, but one is never offered an insight into why she abandoned her ideals in favor of Cesare's, beyond mere resigned capitulation to avoid strife. There is never a hint of an inner process of change; there is only the juxtaposition of her earlier values and those she adopted to please Cesare. In addition, the use of apostrophe loses its effectiveness by dint of sheer overuse. Not far into the novel, the reader wearies of the device and begins to perceive it as artificial, especially when the device is used solely as a carrier of background information.

Cesare is a man with many failings, especially with regard to women. A reader familiar with Saliha Scheinhardt's earlier works may ask why, after portraying so many women victimized by a society that ranks men above women, she chooses as the hero of her latest novel a man who, despite his avowed love for his wife, nonetheless forbids her out of jealousy to wear a certain blouse for fear it will make her too attractive to other men (111). Scheinhardt's reasons for taking care to point out Cesare's flaws may have been that it was important not to paint a portrait of a hero, but rather to depict a man with all human qualities, including weaknesses. This justification does not reconcile the discrepancy in the character of Maria, however, and alienates a reader looking for insight into the couple's relationship. Mere national-cultural differences alone cannot account for the discrepancy.

The element of otherness is underscored by Scheinhardt herself, not only in her self-proclaimed mission of bringing emotion to the dried-up souls that populate the German literary milieu, but also by the choice of subject matter: *Von der Erde bis zum Himmel Liebe* is situated in an unspecified, slightly undeveloped country, the protagonists have vaguely, yet inconsistently, Spanish- or Italian-sounding names and thus the plot is distant from her German-reading public. Her political involvement does not reach into the German milieu beyond documenting, under literary pretexts (*Frauen, die sterben, ohne daß sie gelebt hätten* is one example), injustices to non-Germans in the Federal Republic. One wonders when she will turn her gaze on occurrences of injustice elsewhere in the Federal Republic. The main character, Cesare, was based in actuality on a Turkish publisher, presumably a friend of Scheinhardt's. A reader familiar with Turkey, or even a reader familiar with the descriptions of that country from Scheinhardt's earlier works, will not be surprised by this information, though it is withheld in the book itself, for Scheinhardt has not taken pains to disguise the country as she did the nationality of her characters. Scheinhardt, despite decades of residence in the Federal Republic, chooses to focus primarily on political injustices outside that country's borders. Why does she not speak to injustices in the so-called mainstream of Germany? Why is her position, and above all her perspective as a foreigner, so inextricably bound with her works?

Aysel Özakin also makes her status as a foreigner pivotal in her works. These two women, who came to Germany as adults, not speaking German, understandably felt keenly the alienation experienced by thousands of their compatriots who came as *Gastarbeiter*. Scheinhardt worked for a time on a factory assembly line before her German improved sufficiently for her to pursue an academic career. In contrast, Özakin, the granddaughter of an Ottoman princess, was an established writer in Turkey prior to her arrival, where she lived in the artist's colony of Worpswede in far northern Germany. The publications she produced in the early eighties were translations into German, but more recent texts such as the volume of poetry titled *Zart erhob sie sich bis sie flog* are written in German. The foreword to *Zart erhob sie sich bis sie flog* is dedicated to her grandmother and to Özakin's own new language. Like many of her Turkish literary predecessors in Germany, Özakin first takes stock of her *Werdegang*, her process of development, and like her fellow

Turks, she sees herself as a piece of Turkish history and recollects childhood and family memories. Soon she abandons the
overridingly autobiographical and turns to the symbolic: In
recounting an incident in which, as in many others, her grandmother plays a large role, Özakin moves to larger issues that are
both current and timeless, when she asks in the final line of the
poem whether old follows the new or whether new follows the
old (13).

   While Özakin has no real reason to have personally empathized with the *Gastarbeiter*, the reader is nonetheless struck by
the absence of that particular element in her work. Rather than
emphasize it, she highlights its opposite, the host, or in her case,
hostess. The hosts to *Gastarbeiter* are Germans, and again,
Özakin takes a different angle by choosing to focus on the host
as Turkish and as a woman. The hostess is a transmutable figure,
neither always urban nor rural, sometimes the grandmother,
sometimes a friend, but the qualities she exhibits are constant:
love, warmth, security. The contrast evident to a reader familiar
with the portrayal of the hosts to Turks in the Federal Republic
is stark. Thus, it seems that her treatment of this aspect of the
Gastarbeiter is achieved by inference, actually by omission alone.

   The theme of *Zart erhob sie sich bis sie flog* is adjustment and
survival. Unlike many first-generation writers, Özakin points to
the changes from within, since changes from without are not
forthcoming. Her own grandmother went from wealth to welfare during the course of her life (7), but as Özakin points out in
one of her shorter, but all the more poignant poems, the forced
adjustment enrichened her (21).

   Aysel Özakin's laudatio of her grandmother in this volume
is more than merely sentimental. The figure of the grandmother
symbolizes the long-standing Turkish culture, the pride of
Turkish heritage. Özakin warns against neglecting that culture,
and in saying that a life devoid of cultural heritage may have a
future, but no past, she is also speaking an admonition, an
encouragement to the Turks in Germany whose legacy is rightly
their strength (25).

   Although Özakin chooses in the above-cited works not to

turn her attention to topics specifically dealing with the lives of Turks in the Federal Republic, she does deal with elements of strangeness, emigration, and integration in her poems; it is in her new country that she writes poems of memory and longing about her homeland, embodied in the figure of her grandmother. Childhood is Turkey; adulthood is the West (40). And she neatly dismisses the idea of adjustment to outward surroundings in a short sentence that sums up an adaptive attitude characteristic of many authors whose goal is literary, not sociological, emphasis, when she says she has left what was and thus become integrated within herself (40). She prefers instead to address herself to human universals, and instead of dwelling on differences, she shows her reader universalities. *Zart erhob sie sich bis sie flog* draws to its close with the death of her beloved grandmother, yet after one poem, Özakin shifts the perspective from that death to the demise of an old Dutch woman (50). Universal similarities make the distinctions paltry by comparison, since life, the act of living, accords us equal status with one another.

Aysel Özakin rebels literarily against the constraints she senses in her life as a Turk, and as an author. The former is depicted vividly in poem Number 32 (56).

That text combines her limitations as a Turk with her freedom as a writer in a remarkable contrast that lends pathos to both situations. This woman is an author who has learned to value freedom in every facet of her life, since it was her writing that caused her persona non grata status in Turkey, which in turn led her to go into exile. *"Ich bin ein Erdbewohnerin"* (57) is her answer to Europeans who ask her if she feels like a European, though in the final poem of the volume, she admits that she sees herself as a river that has left its source (57). This book must be interpreted as her statement of displacement, but it cannot be denied that Aysel Özakin's dislocation has had fruitful literary results.

Another woman writer whose life has been marked by personal exile is Zehra Çirak. The bewildering labyrinth of syntax and semantics in her poem "deutsche sprache gute sprache"

mentioned in the previous chapter could be interpreted as bearing witness to her own bewilderment; her own struggle with a language that is not the language spoken in her home, but rather the language of the outside world, of the Other. Çirak came to Germany at the tender age of three, when her father relocated his family from its native Istanbul to Karlsruhe to work in a plant there. The children were raised in strict Islamic piousness, and from this separation of cultures nothing but a sense of displacement could be expected in the children, particularly in the eldest, Zehra.

What does the listener now expect to hear? A litany of woes, of difficulties in reconciling one disparate cultural milieu with an equally strong, albeit subculture? A recounting of the losing battle to find parity between two structurally dissimilar tongues? Narratives of racial slurs? Despair at trying to exist in two worlds at the same time? Resignation? Rage?

The answer evident in the ever-increasing body of poetry, and the smaller but equally significant amount of prose written by Çirak is a subtly but decidedly articulated "NO." The labyrinth of "german language good language" may certainly be a maze of meaning, but it is one that is possible only when constructed by a mind capable of plumbing its depths and mastering its enigma.

In plain English: Çirak is not hampered by her irrefutably displaced status. Rather, her art is made possible by the very element in her existence that, by rights, should cause her the most distress. Just as she refuses to be relegated to one category, *verschubladisiert*, as she puts it, so too does she decline even to see herself as displaced, and in an interview with the Berlin magazine *zitty* in June 1989, she spoke almost disparagingly of her first attempts at poetry (17). German was the language of her diary then to prevent parental eyes from decoding her private thoughts. Perhaps that is one reason why she now dislikes *Betroffenheitsliteratur*. Still, she allows that an author must write from the soul (17).

In rejecting the conventional, that is, negative, definition of displacement for her own, Çirak interprets it in a positive manner and construes from it a state of liberty rather than of isolation. Accordingly, she displaces herself purposely and revels in that status and in the artistic license it affords her. In the laudatory address given for her in January 1989 in Munich, Jürgen Walter, who executed the illustrations for her first volume of poetry, *flugfänger*, reminded the audience of Çirak's wish to sleep on a Japanese futon, to awaken to an English breakfast, followed by a Bavarian *Wanderung*, and to close her intercultural day with African dancing. In short, she, and through her her texts, dreams of abolition of boundaries, of an auspicious and conscious displacement that would ideally shake her readers out of their cultural sloth. A recent poem further illustrates her sentiments. In one text, she portrays poetry not only as universal through the choice of names from A to Z from all over the globe (though notably without reference to geographic location), but as universally human in cause (domestic, political, emotional or personal) and intent (catharsis, reform, pleasure, atonement, success): Each poet is a facet to the common facade of what makes up poetry.

Despite her choice of poetry itself as a topic for a poem, Zehra here further demonstrates her determination not to let herself be locked into rigidity, be it culturally or aesthetically. Even vis-à-vis her forte of literature, she distances herself just as she distances herself from being labeled. For while she praises the broad scope of poetry throughout the world, she cannot resist sly pokes at both poet and craft. Some poets are prima donnas who claim to need certain surroundings, others write only titles and never get past that task to actually write poems, yet others write in order to be successful or to gain admirers, and still others wallow in self-indulgence from the safety of their boudoirs. Thus, while praising poetry's existence, she also wags a finger at it irreverently. In a similar vein, she takes her successes with a grain of salt, knowing that the proof of quality does not always lie in the plaudits given it. The poem she read at the ceremony for the Adelbert von Chamisso Fellowship, funded by the Robert Bosch Foundation and awarded by the Institute of German As a Foreign Language of the University of Munich and the Bavarian Academy of Fine Arts in early 1989 expresses this sentiment in typical Çirakian fashion. This is very likely the first time hairspray has been used as a metaphor for praise!

One other poem by Çirak demonstrates her lack of respect for cultural deities; an irreverence that puts established and idolized literary works to new usage. The cadences, mountain setting, and wanderer hearken back to Goethe, the title reminds the reader of Remarque's *Im Westen nichts Neues*, and the image of flies at the window as a symbol for death is an obvious allusion to Borchert's *Draußen vor der Tür*. The twists of word and plot, however, are quintessentially Çirak.

In seeking the liberty of displacement for herself, Çirak ultimately wishes to bestow it on her readers. Displacement may afford her freedom, but it has its disadvantages: Once, while guest of the Goethe Institute in Ankara, she was accused by Turkish students of being a traitor to her people for not addressing herself more consistently and directly to the situation of Turks in the Federal Republic. But as she says, she seeks discussion—*Auseinandersetzung*—with a wider realm of writers and subjects; the so-called problem of Turks in Germany cannot command her entire concentration. Many of her most recent texts in *Fremde Flügel auf eigener Schulter do* focus on the themes of nationality, nationalism, and xenophobia.

She consciously seeks to displace herself linguistically and semantically, as well as geographically and culturally. Her poems are often witty to the point of being wicked, and generally the *Bissigkeit* is achieved through clever manipulation of the images and expectations that language fosters in its readers and listeners. Although she initially refused to acknowledge any usefulness in the trend toward *Betroffenheitsliteratur*, she saw in the boom of interest in foreigners and their literature not only a chance to be published on a wider scale but also the potential to counteract the litarary ghetto that resulted. The relatively few texts by Çirak that deal with the life of *Gastarbeiter* have an edge to them, and confront the topic from unusual angles. The German *du kannst mich mal*, meaning "you can kiss my ass" is the twist upon which the seemingly inocuous lines about *Gastarbeiter* from the poem—"an den grenzen der gastfreundlichkeit"—from her *flugfänger* volume—are based (17).

To discuss Çirak's texts is to become, as a reader, displaced. The German-speaking reader finds language set on its edge, reoriented as it were, and the resultant shift in perspective leaves the reader with a slightly befuddling, but all the more refreshing, impression of being realigned in relationship to one's own native tongue. Zehra calls her texts language pictures—*Sprachbilder*— and, as she said in the interview with *zitty*, they allow her to incorporate parts of the very figurative Turkish language into her German texts (17). The poem "währung" from *flugfänger* is a perfect example of a language picture; it manipulates language playfully, even while conjuring out of words an image that is quite easy to imagine visually (33).

Chapter Eight

Conclusion: *"Ich glaube fast, ich bin ein deutscher Dichter"*

Like the man to whom the above quote is attributed, Adelbert von Chamisso, the Turkish writers in the Federal Republic are non-native Germans who choose the German language over their native tongue for their literature. And like Chamisso, a French nobleman who emigrated to Germany, and not only changed his name from Louis Charles Adélaïde Chamisso de Boncourt to Adelbert von Chamisso, but also found his muse as a poet when he transferred his linguistic allegiance from French to German, the Turkish writers in the Federal Republic have also found a German-speaking muse. Harald Weinrich compares them to Chamisso in a collection of essays he compiled on foreigners' literature titled *Chamissos Enkel*. They could express the same sentiment as Chamisso, but only if one modification, one amendment is made to allow the above statement to read: "a German-*speaking* poet" (11).

During the proceedings of the March 1988 Evangelische Akademie conference in Iserlohn on the subject of literature in an intercultural context, Gino Chiellino made an impassioned plea to the reading public and to members of the literary scene in Germany on behalf of other foreign writers: He spoke vehemently against being incorporated into the mainstream, the so-called "German" literature.

Thus, any discussion of non-native German literature may not be subsumed under the catch-all label of "German literature," lest this labeling cause a complacent, patronizing attitude in the readership and a sense of inadequacy among writers of non-native German origins themselves. Harald Weinrich, whose work with the Institute for German Foreign Language in Munich has aligned him with those promoting non-native German literature, nonetheless makes an unwitting faux pas in his comment on this area of contemporary literature in Germany—printed in the *Zeitschrift für Kulturaustausch*—when he says it is a province of German literature (15). Not only must he be contradicted, but corrected: A more fitting label for the literature is simply "German-language literature." To label it thus is not mere hairsplitting; it is precision. The label permits the literature of nonnative Germans who *do* write in that tongue to have equal footing with native writers.

In the course of the development of the literature, other labels may have been useful, if not always appropriate. The labels were short-lived, since the shape of what they described changed quickly and frequently, and the descriptors often seemed as limited as they were limiting. Now that the literature itself is expanding to encompass many subjects other than work, oppression and xenophobia, it is time to utilize a label that can accommodate that broad scope. As Zafer Senocak puts it in "Ein Plädoyer für eine Brückenliteratur," his contribution to *Eine nicht nur deutsche Literatur*, the second generation should no longer be categorized under the same label as the writers who came earlier, because the former are transcending every thematic limitation (67).

Like Özakin's intention in *"Ali hinter den Spiegeln,"* the goal of this book has been to look beyond the face that defines Turks, both *Gastarbeiter* and writers, only as sufferers, victims. Pity, says Özakin, is not enough: Does the young German Left, that feels itself to be free of guilt and that is looking for a new social identity, feel nothing but pity toward minorities? (35). At the same time, Özakin rejects any impulse to protect the minority to the extent that its literature is shielded from genuine examination. And this literature, especially in its most recent manifestations, does not seek to ignore the difficulties of the life of the migrants or the double burden of Turkish women, but rather, according to Özakin, resolves to depict reality in all its contradictions and individuality (35).

A sharp contrast to Özakin is Akif Pirinçci, a young writer who purposely puts himself beyond the scope of *any* foreigner's literature. He was asked by the editors of the *Zeitschrift für Kulturaustausch* to participate in the compilation of an issue, and turned down the offer much as he turned down the suggestion that he be aligned with foreigners' literature when interviewed for *Die Zeit*, saying the topic was passé. (32) He keeps himself haughtily aloof from both Turks and Germans, saying he creates his own culture (35). Subsequently, he receives little or no mention in sources dealing with the Turks as writers. He has not given up on literature, however, despite his professed disinterest in words (32). No reference to Pirinçci has appeared in the secondary literature since the appearance of the *Zeitschrift für Kulturaustausch*, but at that time he spoke of his wish to write for films in the future. That wish has been fulfilled; after publishing the little-known novel *Tränen sind immer das Ende*, he struck home with the thriller, *Felidae*. Both novels appeared in the Goldmann publishing house, a publisher primarily characterized by its light-weight literature, joke books, and cartoon books, but the latter, *Felidae*, is an ambitious work. It is replete with footnotes citing scientific and zoological sources on the topic of the work's subjects: cats. Pirinçci's cat mystery novel—*Katzenkrimi*—as the bookjacket describes it, was a great success, and is currently being filmed as a feature-length cartoon. The language of the novel is elaborate, and aspires to be witty, educated, and colorful all at once; in short, it is a perfect book on which to base a film. The narrator speaks in the first person, and even the readers who are not informed about Pirinçci's aspirations can almost hear the *sotto voce* voice-over of a movie hero recounting his story as the reels whirr. The novel is very entertaining and is constructed to keep the reader in suspense and interested until the last word. Pirinçci is an able writer of lively narrative, whose talents seem customized for the screen-writer's *metier*. He can capture an audience quickly and capably, as the opening sentences to *Felidae* demonstrate. In just a few lines, readers find their curiosity piqued and their ear delighted by the slightly pedantic and insistent voice of the narrator, a cat named Frances, who warns that his is no easy story to hear, but that it must be told (1).

Pirinçci holds his reading audience in thrall with these sentences much as authors in earlier eras and with other genres do. Despite the modern setting full of computer data bases, genetic engineering based on Gregor Johann Mendel's study of peas, and passing mention of items peculiar to the 1980s, such as "Miami Vice," the Gothic suspense of the first-person narrative, and floridly elegant speech used in addressing the reader, all hearken back to a different era. Despite the apparent goal of the author to merely entertain, there is a moral to this modern-day Aesop's work. One element of his novel is oddly out of alignment with its pointedly non-intellectual facade: The main character, Francis, a young American shorthair cat—perhaps a modern-day *Kater Murr*—that stumbles upon a dead feline corpse shortly after moving with his owner into their new abode, is given to profoundly philosophical musings on the nature of religion, humankind, and societal hierarchies. It would seem that Pirinçci does have a message hidden in the rather lowbrow focus of the plot.

His characters, except for a few peripheral humans, are cats: cats from all races and genetic backgrounds. The villain of the novel, Claudandus, is a feline Hitler, who seeks racial purity, either by winning over others to his way of thinking, or if necessary, by killing all male or female cats of unpure breeding (242).

The goal of the murderer is dominance over humans, since the humans have gotten away from their original animal integrity. He says that animals are good people and people, bad animals (277). His message seems to stem from an anti-vivisectionist and animal-rights perspective, and the murderer condemns humans, because they oppressed, or better yet, killed other creatures without scruple or shame. It was their self-confidence that gave them the will and the strength for it (260).

Beneath the surface interpretation of a direct application of the plot to real life, it seems quite possible that Pirinçci's message is a more global one—equality and humaneness—that can be applied to his fellow Turks. Surely a young man who grew up witnessing the injustice and struggle for an equal place in German society on the part of the *Gastarbeiter* would take a strong interest not only in Germany's past racist tendencies, but in tendencies of like nature, recent past and present, since, as he has said, the situation of the minorities in German is well known by all.[1]

Pirinçci differs from his peers in the literary scene of second-generation Turks who write in German by being the only one to date to have written a long prose work. Poetry is the preferred genre. Several have mentioned their plans and desires to write novels, but thus far, no one has.

To interpret Pirinçci's novel solely in a biographical light, that is, as a Turk in Germany, does him an injustice. The future of Germany's Turkish writers lies less in their nationality than in their talents. If they prefer to identify themselves as Turkish writers first, and authors second, they are fated to suffer literary marginality. If they can persuade the reading public to accord their identity as Turks less significance in favor of their individual identities as novelists, poets, and satirists, they will outlast the short-lived interest from a reading public solely interested in the novelty of reading a foreigner's works.

Up to now, neither the German public nor scholars of German literature have consistently accorded them the interest that is their due. Especially the second generation has been stigmatized by the image the reading public has of the earlier or first-generation writers whose works were more autobiographical in content. Indeed, had the publishers *not* sought to capitalize on the novelty of the *Gastarbeiter* writing about their existence, the natural progression into wider areas of subject matter and further development of the craft of writing might have occurred sooner. The readers who now sniff disdainfully at foreigners' works are in part to blame for that particular category's development.

Germany must face the reality that, as a country, it is fast becoming multinational, and, subsequently, that the literary scene consists of many subcategories, not of *one* primary category. Until that time, German-speaking readers are unwittingly withholding from themselves a vast scope of writers and topics available in their own country.

To classify writers by nationality alone is to truly judge a book by its cover. When the time comes that readers, publishers, and booksellers overcome the urge to classify primarily by nationality, then—although a work such as this may be unnecessary at best, and, at worst, no longer pertinent—writers will become known by dint of their works alone, instead of for their national origins. Fortunately, to judge by the universality of topics chosen by writers of the second generation, the time seems to be dawning when they can begin not only to escape their current marginality, but also to gain access to the power of influence and the ability to instruct that is ascribed to all writers by Friedrich the Great in the October/November 1985 issue of *Die Brücke* on the occasion of *PoliKunst*'s fifth anniversary: Writers are the law-givers of humanity, revealing the ideas through which others are fulfilled (38).

NOTES

1. Other novels by Pirinççi also deal with facism: *Der Rumpf* and *Frances: Felidae II.*

Bibliography

40 M 2 Deutschland . Dir. Tefvik Beser. 1985.

Abadan-Unat, Nermin. "Die Auswirkungen der internationalen Arbeitsemigration auf die Rolle der Frau am Beispiel der Türkei." Abadan-Unat, 201–237.

———. Ackermann, Irmgard, ed. *Als Fremder in Deutschland*. Munich: Deutscher Taschenbuch Verlag, 1983.

———. "In der Fremde hat man eine dünne Haut." Lorenz and Pazarkaya, 28–32.

———, ed. *In zwei Sprachen leben*. Munich: Deutscher Taschenbuch Verlag, 1983.

———, ed. *Türken deutscher Sprache*. Munich: Deutscher Taschenbuch Verlag.

Ackermann, Irmgard and Harald Weinrich, eds. *Eine nicht nur deutsche Literatur*. Munich: R. Piper, 1986.

Aglaster, Amand. Personal interview. 24 March 1988.

Akpinar, Ünal. "Ausländererlaß...das Mitteilungsblatt zur Pressekonferenz," 2–22.

———, ed. *INFO Zur Pädagogischen Arbeit mit ausländischen Kindern*. Berlin: Zentral Institut für Unterrichtswesen und Curriculum–entwicklung, Sommersemester, 1982.

Aktoprak, Levent. "Entwicklung." Lorenz and Pazarkaya, 143.

Arig, Fatma. Turcan, 50.

Atacan, Ihsan. "Begnungen." Ackermann, *Türken*, 26.

———. "Hängebrücke." Ackermann, *In zwei Sprachen*, 218–221.

Bakirdögen, Ayhan. Mert, *Brücke*, No. 44, August/September, 1988, 57.

———. "Saliha Scheinhardt." Mert, *Brücke* No. 44, 57.

Barin, Ertunç. "Der Aufsatz oder Geständnisse eine 'Gastarbeiter'-Kindes." Ackerman, *In zwei Sprachen*, 127–132.

Baumgartner-Karabak, Andrea and Gisela Landesberger. *Die verkauften Bräute* . Reinbek bei Hamburg: Rowohlt Taschenbuch Verlag, 1986.

Biondi, Franco and Rafik Schami. "Literatur der Betroffenheit." *Schaffernicht* , 136.

Brandt, Ursula. "Türkische Schriftstellerin als deutsche Stadtschreiberin." Sozial-Report. Frankfurt am Main: INP, 2.1. 1986. No. 55.

Çakir, Sabri. "Ich habe zwei Heimatländer." Ackermann, *In zwei Sprachen* , 126.

Çaliskan, Deniz. "Abschied." Ackermann, *Türken* , 33.

Chiellino, Gino. Personal Interview. 19 March 1988.

Çirak, Zehra. Personal interview. 18 January 1988.

Çirak, Zehra. Letter to the author. 1 December 1988.

————. Letter to the author. 4 February 1989.

————. Letter to the author. 25 October 1989.

————. Letter to the author. 13 October 1989.

————. "Brief an meine Schwestern in meinen Heimaten." Lorenz and Pazarkaya, 145–146.

————. *flugfänger*. Karlsruhe: edition artinform, 1987.

————. "nicken mit dem kopf heißt nein." Hölzl and Torossi, 49.

————. "deutsche sprache gute sprache." Janetzki and Zimmermann, 42.

Denizeri, Birol. "Tote Gefühle." Ackermann, *In zwei Sprachen*, 176.

Dewran, Hasan. "An den Ufern des Euphrats." Ackermann, *Türken*, 11.

Die Ausländerbeauftragte des Senats beim Senator für Gesundheit und Soziales, ed. *Miteinander leben*. Berlin: Die Ausländerbeauftragte des Senats beim Senator für Gesundheit und Soziales, 1986.

Die Kümmeltürkin geht. Dir. Jeanine Meerapfel. Berlin, 1985.

Dikmen, Sinasi. *Wir werden das Knoblauchkind schon schaukeln*. Berlin: EXpress Edition, 1987.

Emre, Gültekin. "Aus der Geschichte der Türken in Berlin." Turcan, *Brücke*, September 1987, 16.

Engin, Osman. "Türkischer Brummschädel." Esselborn, *Grenzen*, 100–102.

Über Grenzen. ed. Karl Esselborn. Munich: Deutscher Taschenbuch Verlag, 1987.

Federal Republic of Germany, Commissioner for Foreigners' Affairs of the Senate of Berlin. *Foreign Nationals and Policy of Matters Concerning Foreigners*. 1985, 1.

Franger, Gaby. *Wir haben es uns anders vorgestellt*. Frankfurt am Main: Fischer Taschenbuch Verlag, 1984.

Frederking, Monika. *Schreiben gegen Vorurteile*. Berlin: EXpress Edition, 1985.

Friedrich, Heinz, ed. *Chamissos Enkel*. Munich: Deutscher Taschenbuch Verlag, 1986.

Füruzan. *Logis im Land der Reichen*. Munich: Deutscher Taschenbuch Verlag, 1985.

Halici, Nihat and Semra Aktas. "Knobi-Bonbon Kabaret." Turcan, *Bizim* No. 47, 1989, 40.

Hamm, Horst. *Fremdgegangen, freigeschrieben*. Würzburg: Königshausen und Neumann, 1988.

Heinze, Hartmut. *Migrantenliteratur in der Bundesrepublik*. Berlin: EXpress Edition, 1986.

Hennig, Jörg Erich Straßner and Rainer Roth, eds. *Sprache in der Gesellschaft*. Frankfurt am Main: Verlag Peter Lang, 1984.

Hölzl, Luisa and Elena Torossi, eds. *Freihändig auf dem Tandem*. Kiel: Neuer Malik Verlag, 1985.

HSM. "Zwischen zwei Stühlen." Ackermann, *In zwei Sprachen*, 14.

Janetzki, Ulrich and Lutz Zimmermann, eds. *Anfang sein für einen neuen Tanz kann jeder Schritt*. Berlin: Literarisches Colloqium Berlin, 1988.

Kartal, Hatice and Hülya Özkan. "Sehnsucht." Ackermann, *Als Fremder* 26.

Keskin, Hakki. *Die Zeit*. 17 January 1986, 37.

Kip, Cengiz. "Fahrt der Hoffnungen." Ackermann, *In zwei Sprachen*, 198–202.

König, Karen and Hanne Straube, eds. *Kalte Heimat*. Reinbek bei Hamburg: Rowohlt Taschenbuch Verlag, 1984.

Kuper, Rosemarie. Nachwort. *Logis im Land der Reichen*. By Füruzan. Munich: Deutscher Taschenbuch Verlag 1985, 147–154.

Kurt, Kemal. Personal interview. 27 January 1988.

Kurt, Kemal. *beim nächsten ton*. Berlin: Edition Mariannenpresse, 1988.

———. *Bilder einer Kindheit*. Berlin: EXpress Edition, 1986.

———. "Das Epos vom mustergültigen Ausländerle." Ackermann, *Türken* 87–88.

———. "'schuldigung." Ackermann, *Türken* 226.

———. "Südafrika ist ein fernes Land." Ackermann, *Türken* 230.

Lange, Claudio. "Arbeitsgruppe Literatur." Schwenke and Winkler-Pöhler, 137.

Lernen in Deutschland. Januar 1986, 22–36.

Lorenz, Günter W. and Yüksel Pazarkaya, eds. *Zeitschrift für Kulturaustausch* No. 35. Stuttgart: Institut für Auslandsbeziehungen, 1985.

Lundt, Peter-Michael. *Türken in Berlin*. Berlin: Ausländerbeauftragte beim Senator für Gesundheit und Soziales, 1987.

Mert, Necati, ed. *Die Brücke* No. 44, August/September 1988.

———, ed. *Die Brücke*. No. 57, June/July, 1987.

Ney, Norbert. *Sie haben mich zu einem Ausländer gemacht...* Reinbek bei Hamburg: Rowohlt Taschenbuch Verlag, 1986.

Ören, Aras. *Deutschland, ein türkisches Märchen*. Frankfurt am Main: Fischer Taschenbuch Verlag, 1982.

———. *Die Fremde ist auch ein Haus*. Berlin: Rotbuch Verlag, 1980.

———. *Mitten in der Odyssee*. Frankfurt am Main: Fischer Taschenbuch Verlag, 1983.

———. *Paradies kaputt*. Munich: Deutscher Taschenbuch Verlag, 1986.

———. *Privatexil*. Berlin: Rotbuch Verlag, 1977.

———. *Was will Niyazi in der Naunynstraße*. Berlin: Rotbuch Verlag, 1980.

Özakin, Aysel. "Ali Hinter den Spiegeln." Schwenke and Winkler-Pöhler, 32–36.

———. *Zart erhob sie sich bis sie flog*. Hamburg: Verlag am Galgenberg, 1986.

Özkan, Hülya. "Zukunft ohne Gegenwart." Ackermann, *In zwei Sprachen*, 111.

Pazarkaya, Yüksel. "deutsche sprache." Lorenz and Pazarkaya, 144.

———. "Stimme des Zorns und der Einsamkeit in Bitterland." Lorenz and Pazarkaya, 16–28.

Picardi-Montesardo. *Die Gastarbeiter in der Literatur der Bundesrepublik Deutschland*. Berlin: EXpress Edition, 1985.

Pirinçci, Akif. *Felidae*. Munich: Goldmann Verlag, 1989.

———. *Tränen sind immer das Ende*. Munich: Goldmann Verlag, 1988.

Reeg, Ulrike. *Schreiben in der Fremde*. Essen: Klartext, 1988.

Riemann, Wolfgang. *Das Deutschlandbild in der modernen türkischen Literatur*. Wiesbaden: Otto Harrassowitz, 1983.

Rösch, Heidi. Personal Interview. 28 June 1988.

Savasçi, Özgür. "An die Isar." Ackermann, *Türken*, 111.

———. "An einem Freitagabend." Ackermann, *In zwei Sprachen*, 92.

Scheinhardt, Saliha. Personal Interview. 24 June 1988.

———. *Drei Zypressen*. Berlin: EXpress Edition, 1984.

———. *Frauen, die sterben, ohne daß sie gelebt hätten*. Berlin: EXpress Edition, 1983.

———. *Träne für Träne werde ich heimzahlen*. Reinbek bei Hamburg: Rowohlt, 1987.

———. *Und die Frauen weinten Blut*. Berlin: EXpress Edition, 1985.

———. *Von der Erde bis zum Himmel Liebe*. Frankfurt am Main/Wien: Büchergilde Gutenberg, 1988.

Schierloh, Heimke. "Das alles für ein Stück Brot." Hennig, Straßner and Roth, *Sprache*, 11–44.

Schleyer, Walter. "Aus der Diskussion." Schleyer, *Informationen*, 272–291.

———, ed. *Informationen Deutsch als Fremdsprache*. Munich: iudicium, No. 3, June 1985.

Schwenke, Olof and Beate Winkler-Pöhler, eds. *Loccumer Protokolle* (03/87).

Seidel-Pielen, Eberhared. *zitty*. Berlin: zitty Verlag, No 6, 1989, 17.

Sen, Suhan. "Einladung." Ackermann, *Als Fremder*, 117.

Senocak, Zafer. "Doppelmann." Ackermann, *Türken*, 39.

———. "Du bist ein Arbeitsknochen." Ackermann, *Türken*, 89–90.

———. "Ohne Grenzen." Ackermann, *Türken*, 245.

Suhr, Heidrun. Rev. of *Schreiben in der Fremde* by Ulrike Reeg. *German Quarterly* 62, No. 4, 1989, 562–563.

Schwenke, Olof, and Beate Winkler-Pöhler, eds. "Kulturelles Wirken in einem anderen Land." *Loccumer Protokolle*. Loccum: Evangelische Akademie, 1987.

Tekinay, Alev. "Ali Stern." Ackermann, *In zwei Sprachen*, 132–136.

———. "Die Heimkehr oder Tante Helga und Onkel Hans." Ackermann, *Türken*, 40–51.

———. "Langer Urlaub." Ackermann, *In zwei Sprachen* 203–213.

———. "Muammer Tuksavul." Turcan, *Bizim*, February 1986, 48.

Timur, Serim. "Charakteristika der Familienstruktur in der Türkei." Abadan-Unat, *Die türkische Frau*, 56.

Turcan, Tuba, ed. *Bizim Almanca/Unser Deutsch*. Istanbul: Cagdas Yayincilik ve Basin Sanayii, No. 8, November 1985.

———, ed. *Bizim* No. 11.

———, ed. *Bizim* No. 30.

"'Türkisch gedacht, deutsch geschrieben'." Hanauer Anzeiger. 3.29.1986, Hanau-Land, 11.

Üçüncü, Sadi. *Freund, gib mir deine Hand*. Altenberge: CIS-Verlag, 1986.

von Schirnding, Albert. "Die zweite Geburt." *Süddeutsche Zeitung*. 27 February 1989, 32.

Wallraff, Günter. *Ganz unten*. Berlin: Kiepenhauer und Witsch, 1984.

Weinrich, Harald. "Betroffenheit der Zeugen—Zeugen der Betroffenheit." Lorenz and Pazarkaya, *Kulturausch*, 14–15.

Yasmin. Dir. Hark Bohm. Berlin, 1987.

Yilmaz, Oral. "Die zweisprachige Welt." Ackermann, *In zwei Sprachen*, 44.